ESTHER

THE GUIDE

ESTHER

Peter Bloomfield

 EVANGELICAL PRESS

EVANGELICAL PRESS
Faverdale North Industrial Estate, Darlington,
DL3 0PH, England

Evangelical Press USA
P. O. Box 84, Auburn, MA 01501, USA

e-mail: sales@evangelicalpress.org

web: http://www.evangelicalpress.org

First published 2002

**British Library Cataloguing in Publication Data
available**

ISBN 0 85234 509 7

Printed and bound in Great Britain by Creative Print
and Design Wales, Ebbw Vale, South Wales.

CONTENTS

HOW TO USE *THE GUIDE*

Esther is the fourth book in a new series of publications called *The Guide*. This series will cover books of the Bible on an individual basis, such as *Colossians and Philemon*, and relevant topics such as *Christian comfort*. The series aim is to communicate the Christian faith in a straightforward and readable way.

Each book in *The Guide* will cover a book of the Bible or topic in some detail, but will be contained in relatively short and concise chapters. There will be questions at the end of each chapter for personal study or group discussion, to help you to study the Word of God more deeply.

An innovative and exciting feature of *The Guide* is that it is linked to its own web site. As well as being encouraged to search God's Word for yourself, you are invited to ask questions related to the book on the web site, where you will not only be able to have your own questions answered, but also be able to see a selection of answers that have been given to other readers. The web site can be found at www.evangelicalpress.org/ TheGuide. Once you are on the site you just need to click on the 'select' button at the top of the page, according to the book on which you wish to post a question. Your question will then be answered either

by Michael Bentley, the web site co-ordinator and author of *Colossians and Philemon*, or others who have been selected because of their experience, their understanding of the Word of God and their dedication to working for the glory of the Lord.

Ecclesiastes, The Bible book by book, and *Colossians and Philemon* have already been published in this series and many more will follow. It is the publisher's hope that you will be stirred to think more deeply about the Christian faith, and will be helped and encouraged in living out your Christian life, through the study of God's Word, in the difficult and demanding days in which we live.

CHAPTER ONE

CONSPICUOUS BY HIS ABSENCE

BIBLE READING

The book of Esther: an overview

INTRODUCTION

God moves in a mysterious way,
His wonders to perform;
He plants His footsteps in the sea,
And rides upon the storm.

Deep in unfathomable mines
Of never-failing skill,
He treasures up His bright designs,
And works His sovereign will.

This hymn by William Cowper (1731-1800) sums up the message of the book of Esther. The glory of God is all the more conspicuous in Esther because he is not mentioned anywhere! Though the reader cannot miss his invisible hand working out his purposes behind the scenes of human history, God is absent in this book. His name is not mentioned and there are no 'miracles' or 'supernatural' events. There is no reference to prayer, or the law of God. There is no mention of great Jewish patriarchs like Abraham, or heroes like Moses, Joshua, or Elijah. Indeed the Jewish people themselves have almost become anonymous. They chose to remain as the exiled people of God, without temple, priest, or prophet. They did not even have a spiritual leader. And suddenly they are in danger of complete extermination, when the satanic character Haman is given authority to murder every Jew in Persia.

But God's absence only makes him more conspicuous. He works all things according to the counsel of his own will, and this book shows us how the king and his empire are in God's hands, even the king's sleepless nights! God uses the mundane events of everyday human life to accomplish his covenant purposes. Whether it is the heart of a king, the evil malice of a scheming politician, the pretty girls aspiring to become Queen of Persia, or the superstitions of the ancient Near Eastern cultures, all are in the hands of the God of Scripture. He rules and overrules so that when humans do what they truly want to do, they unwittingly accomplish the designs of God; yet he remains the author of only good but never evil.

That is undoubtedly the major impact arising from the book of Esther. It is a wonderful story, brilliantly told by the author. My aim is to show you its great value, although it has not always received a good reception. The Jews who had returned to Palestine after the Babylonian exile did not want to accept this Persian publication into the canon of Scripture (especially since God was not mentioned). Even in the Christian Church it was regarded as unimportant. Not a single commentary was written on Esther for the first seven centuries of the Christian era! Indeed it is not until the sixteenth-century Reformation period that a serious commentary of lasting worth was produced. Even prolific scholars like Martin Luther and John Calvin left no commentaries on Esther.

Esther is a valuable book. The vast majority of Jews never returned to Palestine after Cyrus the Mede set them free. The history of the few who did return is seen in the books of Ezra, Haggai and Nehemiah. But Esther is the only biblical record of what happened to the vast majority of Abraham's descendants who stayed in Persia. Moreover, if the danger shown in Esther had not been overcome by God's providential rule, the vast majority of Jews would have been exterminated. There would have been no Nehemiah and no rebuilt Jerusalem. Worse, there would have been no Jesus!

As we shall see, the villain in this story is Haman, a traditional enemy of God and his covenant people. Haman is the human face of Satan's determination to destroy the promised Saviour, the seed of the woman (Genesis 3:15). Like Pharaoh before him and Herod after him, Haman leads sinful humanity in its attack against God's chosen people from whom Jesus Christ the Saviour would be born. The book of Esther has to be understood as another scene in the ongoing enmity between the seed of the serpent and the seed of the woman. God's plan of salvation was under attack in Persia; but his promises are reliable. He is not really absent here at all. He is absent only in the sense of 'unseen', but that makes him all the more noticeable.

It is good to begin with an overview, taking a panoramic look over the book. This can be done helpfully by summing up the story and setting out the lessons.

Summing up the story

The book begins with the 'mother of all parties' held by the Persian King Ahasuerus (better known as Xerxes, his Greek name).[1] After the first week of this 180-day feast, when the king was affected by wine, he ordered Vashti his Queen to be put on display so that everyone could see her good looks. How vain! But she refused (most readers would say 'Good for you'); and it cost her: she was banished to instant irrelevance. In order to find a new queen a beauty contest was held: 'The Miss Persia Contest 483 BC'! The winner was Esther (this Persian name concealing her Jewish name, *Hadassah*), who had been raised by her cousin Mordecai in the Persian capital Shusan (Susa).

Despite her success in the beauty contest it was four years before Esther was installed as queen. The delay was caused by the king's disastrous attempts to invade Greece. The battles at Thermopylae and Salamis were a nightmare for him, leaving no time to attend to domestic issues.

However, these domestic issues came to the fore when Mordecai overheard a treacherous plot to kill the king. He 'blew the whistle' by telling Esther, who in turn informed the king. The villains were hanged. By an oversight, Mordecai was never rewarded, a fact which becomes important later. Then we meet a most unsavoury wretch, Haman. He is the sort of person whom you dread to see in any position of authority. Put a nametag and uniform on the Hamans of this world and you have an instant tyrant, giddy with power. Haman was made Persia's Chief Minister, answering only to the king himself. As he strutted about the Empire, people were supposed to bow down to Haman; but Mordecai refused. This was not due to any malice or hatred in Mordecai but out of conscience, for Haman was a descendant of the Amalekite king Agag. In other words, he was an inveterate and ancient enemy of Israel. But Haman resented Mordecai's refusal to bow. In an extreme overreaction he determined to murder every single Jew in the empire. As readers, we rightly detect a satanic obsession at work here.

Haman obtained royal consent for this genocidal slaughter, and selected the time by the superstitious casting of the *pur* (the lot, a cube with numbers on it like our dice). The date that came up was the thirteenth day of Adar, the twelfth month. That was eleven months away: eleven months of waiting … eleven months of

hating and seething and loathing Mordecai. But superstitious people would never go against their 'lucky'
numbers! So the chilling decree went out with the
coverage of a CNN News broadcast:

> Dispatches were sent by couriers to all the king's
> provinces with the order to destroy, kill and an-
> nihilate all the Jews — young and old, women
> and little children — on a single day, the thir-
> teenth day of the twelfth month, the month of
> Adar, and to plunder their goods. A copy of the
> text of the edict was to be issued as law in every
> province and made known to the people of every
> nationality so they would be ready for that day
> (3:13-14).

REMEMBER THIS

Even 'chance' events are under God's control:
'The lot is cast into the lap, but its every decision
is from the LORD' (Proverbs 16:33).

In the thick of this crisis Esther's real character
emerges. She knows she must now reveal her Jewish
identity and allegiance. So, by acts of great courage and
masterful wisdom, she (with Mordecai) devised a plan
that not only saved the Jews, and maintained the affec-
tion of the King of Persia, but also destroyed Haman. A
real turning point in the book occurs on a night when
the king could not sleep. Since sleeping pills had not

been invented, he asked for the next best thing: his servants began to read him the royal chronicles (the official history of Persia). Like watching hours of family slides, they were guaranteed to put him to sleep! But God was at work in these mundane circumstances. The king discovered that Mordecai had never been rewarded for saving his life. Meanwhile, Haman arrived at the palace, intending to suggest hanging Mordecai on the gallows he had just built. The king asked his advice on what would be a suitable way to reward a deserving person. Haman gave a pompous answer because he was conceited and arrogant enough to assume that he was that deserving person:

> So he answered the king, 'For the man the king delights to honour, have them bring a royal robe the king has worn and a horse the king has ridden, one with a royal crest placed on its head. Then let the robe and horse be entrusted to one of the king's most noble princes. Let them robe the man the king delights to honour, and lead him on the horse through the city streets, proclaiming before him, "This is what is done for the man the king delights to honour!"' (6:7-9).

What great pleasure the reader gets when Haman is ordered to honour Mordecai in that way. What poetic justice! It couldn't happen to a nicer man! Haman then became extremely anxious, as he 'rushed home, with his head covered, in grief' (6:12). It was all downhill from there. Esther exploited his vanity further by inviting only him and the king to banquets on successive days. How special he felt! He was the only guest of the King and Queen of Persia, two days in a row. But that's where the king learned that Haman had plotted the murder of Queen Esther's people and how he had given his royal authority to it, partly because Haman twisted the truth, partly by his bribery of financial benefits, and certainly by Haman concealing the real reason for his vile plot. While the distressed king went out for some fresh air, a desperate Haman fell down before Queen Esther to plead for his life. From where the king stood, it looked like Haman was sexually molesting her as she reclined on her couch.

Just as the king returned from the palace garden to the banquet hall, Haman was falling on the couch where Esther was reclining. The king exclaimed, 'Will he even molest the queen while she is with me in the house?' As soon as the word left the king's mouth, they covered Haman's face. Then Harbona, one of the eunuchs attending the king, said, 'A gallows seventy-five feet high stands by Haman's house. He had it made for Mordecai, who spoke up to help the king.' The king said, 'Hang him on it!' So they hanged Haman on the

gallows he had prepared for Mordecai. Then the king's fury subsided (7:8-10).

Mordecai replaced Haman as Chief Minister. Since the laws of Medes and Persians are permanent and cannot be revoked, another way was found to save the Jews. They were given permission to defend themselves. They did so very effectively; indeed, as a safety precaution, many Persians became Jews before the big day. The book closes with a short epilogue (chapter 10 has just three verses), which ends with the words: 'Mordecai the Jew was second in rank to King Xerxes, pre-eminent among the Jews, and held in high esteem by his many fellow Jews, because he worked for the good of his people and spoke up for the welfare of all the Jews.' So the purpose of the book is clear: it shows how God raised up the right people at the right time to work for the good of his covenant people who remained outside the promised land.

Setting out the lessons

Events in the book of Esther provide many practical applications for Christians today. We'll see them as we progress, but for now we can learn three significant lessons from the book as an entire unit.

1. Be careful judging a book

To the proverbial truth 'You can't judge a book by its cover' we should add 'You can't judge a book by its omissions.' We are very unwise to downgrade a book just because it is not explicit in saying things that we think it should say. We must not prejudice the value of a spiritual work just because it does not have God's name and God's works stated up-front in flashing lights! Yes, there are situations where subtlety is inappropriate. The thundering judgements of God from heaven are typical. Who can imagine the Exodus literature not naming God right up front? How could the victory song of Moses (Exodus 15) celebrate horses and riders tossed into the sea by 'an unseen hand'? Subtlety would miss the point. And how could the flood of Noah ever be described subtly?

But there are situations where subtlety is called for, where the things implied but not overtly stated add to the impact of the book. Such is Esther. Readers are left to draw their own conclusions that all these remarkable turns of events could never just 'happen'. There is no doubt that the unseen hand of the Almighty is working his purposes out. He is made conspicuous by his absence. It is analogous to those last moments of light at sunset. The sun is no longer visible. It has disappeared below the horizon, but the beautiful effect of a reddish-orange sky playing upon the clouds implies that the sun is still very active! Likewise, God is at work beyond our visible horizon and the glorious effects of that are plain to the eye of a believer, being all the more special because of its subtlety.

To be candid, the common criticisms about the book of Esther are quite artificial and prejudiced. There are good reasons for the writer not littering it with explicit Jewish terms. There are good reasons for omitting direct references to Jehovah, worship, or to prophets and priests. There are good reasons for avoiding the mention of Jerusalem, temple, law, covenant and anything dear to Zion. Yet these should never have been reasons for wanting to leave Esther out of the canon of Scripture. They should never have been reasons for relegating it as 'unimportant' in Christian scholarship for so long. Let us always assume that (all things being equal) an author has the right to get a message across in the manner he or she considers most suitable, and in doing so the author has the right to be considered rational, without the *a-priori* biases and expectations of a reader devaluing the finished product.

2. Be careful judging history

History is a very confusing mosaic of human interactions. We cannot see how it all fits together. Most of us are prone to assess history from a moralistic standpoint. The lessons we extract are moralistic in tone: 'That action is wrong, he shouldn't have done that, and we shouldn't do it either, so take heed.' But in reading the biblical books, that approach is fraught with danger. Scripture is not written as a moralistic history manual. The Bible's approach to history is not moralistic but covenantal. In other words it is showing us how almighty God works in the midst of human intrigue, through all the actions and intentions of men and women, through all the virtuous and non-virtuous thoughts, words and deeds. Regardless of their successes, failures, frustrations, hopes and fears, he infallibly accomplishes his eternal plans and purposes. God rules and overrules to achieve his covenant will in Christ. Nothing can frustrate him. Yet, in all of this, God does not violate or mitigate true human freedom, nor does he depend on it.

So the whole situation in Esther is covenantal. We must avoid being blinkered with the moralistic agenda that has caused many readers to entirely miss its point. There are many moral questions asked: Should these Jews have taken the soft option of remaining in Persia rather than returning to face the risky hard work of rebuilding Zion? Should Esther have agreed to marry a pagan king? Shouldn't Mordecai have obeyed the governing authority by bowing to Haman? Didn't his civil disobedience cause all the trouble? Was it right for Esther and others to hide their Jewish identity? Shouldn't God's people be unashamed to worship him publicly like Daniel did? Should the Jews have killed so many in Haman's pogrom? Wasn't it gruesome to hang Haman's ten sons on the gallows when they were already dead?

Whatever value there is in discussing these moral issues, it is not the purpose of the book. The writer is not wanting us to give a score on a scale from zero to ten for all the moral issues raised. He wants us to see God at work, advancing his great purposes, using ordinary men and women as instruments in all the ordinary scenes of life, both the good and the evil. Always look for the kingdom of God being advanced as you read history. Esther is classic salvation history, redemptive history, not moralistic history.

As a corollary, we should recall that the Jews who had returned to Palestine after the Babylonian captivity tended to disdain the majority who remained in Persia. A rift developed in Judaism. On the one hand there were those Jews who saw themselves as more orthodox, more overtly religious, doing the Lord's work in Israel, in 'full-time service for God'. On the other hand, there were those who were more 'involved in the world' in pagan Persia. These 'holier than thou' views are not dead by any means. But Esther shows the folly of it. God has his purpose exalting some people to prominent places in the seats of worldly power and influence. He is at work in Persia as much as Palestine. He is at work in palaces and politics as well as in temples and seminaries. Christians need to watch the tendency to glorify those who are in 'full-time work' like missionaries and ministers. There is no sacred-secular distinction to justify that. God uses all his people all over the world in all arenas of service to advance his kingdom. Esther is a sober teacher on this matter.

3. God does not forsake his people

Though living in an alien place, the Jews in Persia were still God's people, citizens of the promised land. By analogy, Christians today are true citizens of heaven (Philippians 3:20). We presently live in an alien world where enemies of God (like Haman) rise up against us. We are *in* the world but not *of* the world. We are on the way to the great promised land, the new heavens and new earth. But we are not alone. God is still our shield and defender. He still governs the universe. He still protects his people. 'We know that in all things God works for the good of those who love him' (Romans 8:28). Jesus has promised that, wherever we may go among the nations, he will never forsake us (Matthew 28:20). So the biblical theme of 'Jews in dispersion' stretches beyond Persia in 483 B.C. It included Peter's audience, whom he called 'God's elect, strangers in the world, scattered throughout Pontus, Galatia, Cappadocia, Asia and Bithynia' (1 Peter 1:1). It included the Jews in Egypt and during their journey to the promised land. It really includes all God's people in all of history. From 'paradise lost' in Adam to 'paradise regained' in Christ, God is always preserving his covenant people in their alien lands.

DISCUSS IT

1. Is God's will frustrated by wicked people? See Daniel 4:34-35; Psalm 115:3; and Proverbs 16:1,4,5,9.

2. God, though unseen, is working behind the scenes of human history. How do the following texts encourage us to be always conscious of that? Genesis 50:20; Acts 17:24-31; Romans 9:16-17,19-26; and Ephesians 1:9-11.

3. Why do we need to be careful in judging history? See Romans 11:33-36; 1 Corinthians 13:12.

4. Why is pessimism not an option for Christians? See Romans 8:28; 35-39.

CHAPTER TWO

DRUNKEN
PARANOIA

BIBLE READING

Esther 1

INTRODUCTION

In the opening scene of the book of Esther, we are confronted with the drunken paranoia of the most powerful king on the earth. It happened while he catered to his vanity, showing off before all the military's top brass and the important leaders of his vast empire of 127 provinces. So, 'in the third year of his reign he gave a banquet for all his nobles and officials. The military leaders of Persia and Media, the princes, and the nobles of the provinces were present. For a full 180 days he displayed the vast wealth of his kingdom and the splendour and glory of his majesty' (1:3-4). Then we see an even more obnoxious side to him: 'when King Xerxes was in high spirits from wine, he commanded the seven eunuchs who served him ... to bring before him Queen Vashti ... in order to display her beauty to the people and nobles, for she was lovely to look at. But ... Queen Vashti refused to come. Then the king became furious and burned with anger' (1:10-12).

The reader has little difficulty predicting what happens next, particularly Vashti's exit from the scene. She
is banished to irrelevance. But what the reader could
not predict is the foolish reaction of Xerxes and his
chief advisers. In an empire already besotted with the
rule of law, laws beyond reformation, permanent laws
that could not be revoked or repealed, the reader could
be forgiven for thinking that legislative folly had just
about reached its zenith in the ancient Near East. But
then we learn of a ludicrous new law being decreed. It
is not only the king who manifests paranoid tendencies:
the 'minders' who act as his 'think-tank' moved swiftly
into political damage-control. They show all the classic signs of being diplomatic rather than truthful, re-
sulting in a complete misreading of the likely results
of Vashti's actions. The remedy proposed is yet more
legislation, hastily drafted, acutely reactionary, incap-
able of being policed, and driven by an inebriated
paranoia.

The author acquaints us with this scene in prepar-
ation for our seeing the providential rule of God in
human history. In this messy situation, God rules and
overrules, delivering his covenant people from the terrible threat of extermination about to come upon them.
Almighty God is not frustrated by the actions or
inactions of mere creatures. His purposes will stand
and cannot fail. Neither the malice of a Haman, nor
the drunken paranoia of a powerful king, nor the
political stupidity of the Persian court, can frustrate
the Most High God. That is the issue we must constantly

keep before us as we interpret this book. We can get a good understanding of this opening chapter by considering:

1. The incident (a new law)
2. The issue (insubordination)
3. The irony (intent of author)

The incident

Let's recall the incident. Xerxes asked his advisers, 'According to law, what must be done to Queen Vashti? She has not obeyed the command of King Xerxes that the eunuchs have taken to her' (v. 15). There appears to be no time spent in thought, and no actual exchange of ideas is mentioned. Rather, one man, Memucan, speaks his mind and all the others agree.

Queen Vashti has done wrong, not only against the king but also against all the nobles and the peoples of all the provinces of King Xerxes. For the Queen's conduct will become known to all the women, and so they will despise their husbands and say, 'King Xerxes commanded queen Vashti to be brought before him, but she would not come. This very day the Persian and Median women of the nobility who have heard about the queen's conduct will respond to all the king's nobles in the same way. There will be no end of disrespect and discord. Therefore, if it pleases the king, let him issue a royal decree and let it be written in the laws of Persia and Media, which cannot be repealed, that Vashti is never again to enter the presence of King Xerxes. Also let the king give her royal position to someone else who is better than she. Then when the king's edict is proclaimed throughout all his vast realm, all the women will respect their husbands, from the least to the greatest.' The king and his nobles were pleased with this advice, so the king did as Memucan proposed. He sent dispatches to all parts of the kingdom, to each province in its own script and to each people in its own language, proclaiming in each people's tongue that every man should be ruler over his own household (vv. 16-22).

There are lots of problems here. Notice several features:

1. Diplomatic truth-avoidance

The advice was an astute piece of diplomacy because it took the heat off the king's personal resentment at Vashti's rebuff, setting it into a wider context, making it everyone's problem. 'There will be no end of disrespect and discord ... every family will suffer ... your majesty has good reason to be disturbed, Vashti's rebellion will spread like cancer … the female eunuch has come early!' But like so much diplomacy it carefully avoided the truth. The truth is, Xerxes was a fool to do what he did. He was driven by vanity and inebriation. But if he must indulge himself, why did he command Vashti so publicly? Why order seven messengers to bring her along, even telling her what to wear? Why set himself up for such public humiliation? Why make her refusal a crisis of state? Why did he not simply *request* her attendance and do it privately and discretely? The king should have been confronted with the folly of his actions. But nothing much has changed in the corridors of power: truth is often expendable in politics.

2. Why a new law?

Even with their penchant for diplomacy, why resort to more legislation? Why not simply banish Vashti? Why not let her swift punishment warn everyone that insubordination is not tolerated in Persia? And how on earth will such a law be policed? The new law said 'that every man should be ruler over his own household'. It had all the potential to make the king look like a fool in the eyes of his subjects. Imagine telling each family that every man should be the head of the house! That was already the normal situation anyway. Xerxes has set himself up for their obvious reply: 'You're a fine one to tell us that, a king who couldn't even rule over his own wife!'

In any case, what does that law mean? Does it open the door for men to rule like tyrants so that no woman dare resist? Given faulty human nature, that law would now become very intrusive and very provocative in every household. It would become the cause of endless demarcation disputes and futile arguments in families where peace once prevailed.

3. Biased assessment

Why was their assessment so negative? Why did they consider only the worst scenario? Why think only of Vashti as some sort of cult leader of a 'women strike back' campaign? Why even consider damage control? There was, after all, at least another possible outcome from Vashti's performance: it might signal to husbands everywhere that women are not mindless pieces of property to be bossed around, expected to obey every command, be it in sobriety or drunkenness, virtue or vanity. Women are not trinkets who have, by marriage, forfeited all intellectual independence, yielded up their moral judgements, and sacrificed their consciences on the altar of wedlock. In other words, the practical consequence of this whole incident may well have been that husbands should 'grow up', not that women should 'strike back'. From the facts that we *do* know, that is a far more likely outcome, and very timely still in Iran (formerly Persia).

4. Implicit insult

What an insult is implied to the wives of these Persian officials! Their own husbands don't trust them. Notice the words of the officials: 'The queen's conduct will become known to all the women, and so they will despise their husbands and say, "King Xerxes commanded Queen Vashti to be brought before him, but she would not come." This very day the Persian and Median women of the nobility who have heard about the queen's conduct will respond to all the king's nobles in the same way.' They feared that they would go home to discover they too had married a Vashti! What a low view of your wife! Surely husbands and wives read every day of cases of real treachery and disloyalty in marriages without it affecting their trust in their own spouse. Either these officials had very unhappy homes, or, more likely, they are so entrenched in political face-saving for Xerxes, so immersed in diplomatic expediencies and truth avoidance, that a ludicrous law seems the only way forward.

The issue

As noted already, a moralistic rather than covenantal approach to scriptural books is dangerous. The book of Esther raises a large array of issues for moralistic judgements by those who

are so inclined. But this is redemptive history, salvation history. The author is focusing on the way God
works in history to accomplish his Messianic kingdom.
However, there is so much moralizing regarding Vashti's
insubordination that some comments are needed. The
issue, of course, concerns the woman's role within
marriage as the partner who is submissive to her husband's headship. The biblical ethic is summed up in
Ephesians 5:22-23: 'Wives, submit to your husbands
as to the Lord. For the husband is the head of the wife
as Christ is the head of the church.'

So Vashti is judged as culpable of insubordination.
She is regarded as a rebel, and there is no shortage of
moralistic sermons on marriage preached on Esther 1.
However, there are some difficulties in looking at this
passage in that way.

1. Xerxes' distorted notion of headship

The model of headship taught in Scripture is based on
love, not power. It is a picture of a loving husband
whose concern is for the best interests of his wife.
Proper headship towards a wife is thoughtful, considerate of her person, gracious and self-denying. But
Xerxes was inebriated and proud. The fact is that Vashti
was very beautiful and Xerxes wanted to show her off
too, just as he had done with all his other treasures.
His command to her was unreasonable. For one thing,
he did not consider her responsibilities to the guests
she was entertaining at the time in the palace (v. 9).
Furthermore, he obviously cared nothing for her

WHAT THE TEXT TEACHES

feelings about being paraded before hundreds of men in varying degrees of intoxication, to be put on show like a prize piece of horseflesh. We have already noted the folly of such a public command sent by seven officials to her. If moral blame is being apportioned, we should start with Xerxes. He is very immature, vain, self-centred and was himself inebriated at the time.

2. Be clear on the ethic

The submission God requires of wives is not unlimited. There is no across-the-board obligation for wives to obey every command that a husband utters. The Bible does not teach the notion that a wife is 'the little woman' who must jump to every beck and call of 'him who must be obeyed', even a childish, vain, drunken 'him'. Sadly, there are people who advocate precisely that notion of slavish surrender.[1] What damage they do to the truth! How odious they make the gospel seem. The definitive term in Ephesians 5:22 is 'as to the Lord' or, as Colossians 3:18 has it, 'Wives, submit to your husbands, as is fitting in the Lord.' In other words, her first allegiance is to godly principles. She is to submit in all things consistent with godliness. This is not an excuse for rebellion but a safeguard against foolish headship. A wife is not a slave but a 'suitable helper', a companion.

So let me put the question pointedly. Do you think it is consistent with godliness for a wife to drop what she's doing, come out on show, strut the podium in her fanciest clothes, before the lustful eyes of hundreds of intoxicated men, simply to show that she's the prettiest girl in town, thus making her immature husband's pride tingle? If you think so, then by all means cast your moral judgement against Vashti. Vote against her! But considering all the evidence, she was perfectly within her rights. Moreover, she must have had some inkling of what it would cost her. No Persian queen could be ignorant of the risk involved in refusing the command of a Persian king! So Vashti acted with considerable courage. It may well be that she is to be commended rather than condemned. Moralistic hermeneutics is a very dangerous track to take.

Advice for husbands

The Bible tells husbands: 'be considerate as you live with your wives, and treat them with respect as the weaker partner / vessel' (1 Peter 3:7). This universal 'weakness' of wives cannot be physical, intellectual or moral (some women exceed some men in all of these). It refers to her role. A wife agrees to the supporting role, to follow her man's headship. She willingly takes on the weaker role (that takes strength). So keep that in mind, you

WHAT THE TEXT TEACHES

husbands! How would you like to be in her shoes, submitting to your headship? Be reasonable! Xerxes failed here.

3. Where is the real insubordination?

It is amazing how people focus on minor details and miss the main point. Whatever we think about Vashti's insubordination, it is trivial compared to the universal insubordination of all men and women towards the living God. Here is a whole pagan nation refusing the God who made them. Here is a nation that makes idols and swaps the truth for a lie. Vashti saying 'No' to King Xerxes is trifling compared to humans saying 'No' to God.

The irony

Here I want to assist you to appreciate this book as literature, and skilful literature at that. We have already noted that the author makes no reference to God, but it is a clever way of making the deductions of the reader more telling. Now, in this opening scene, the lavish (even bizarre) situation is described in a low-key way. The author simply describes the events without comment. He avoids character judgements, there are no assessments, no drawing out conclusions or lessons. We are left to make our own deductions.

One of the tools the writer uses to guide us is *irony*.
There are several ironic nuances we should note.

a. Irony of Xerxes. There is an ironic contrast between
King Xerxes at the start and finish of the scene. At the
start he is the world's greatest monarch, rich, powerful, aloof yet generous. But at the end he struggles to
retain any dignity, raging with anger, not even sober,
and his authority is defied by the queen.

b. Irony of law. There are two forms of this. First, there
is the irony of an empire made proverbially famous for
its laws, now over-legislating, and hastily enacting a
silly law. The mentality of Xerxes is 'there should be a
law against it', and it is an easy mentality to get into.
But in fact no society can legislate good citizenship. Of
course, a basic framework of laws is necessary for peace
and justice, but it is a dangerous practice to rely on
law. The health of a society depends on the underlying
character of its citizens, their moral and spiritual qualities, their work ethic and enterprise. Laws cannot
produce these things. The great dangers of over-
legislation are familiar to us all and are well illustrated
in Esther. As usual, the only people to benefit are
lawyers: they laugh all the way to the bank. Litigation
was set to rise after Xerxes' new 'family law' bill.

Second, there is an appealing irony in Vashti being
banished for ignoring the authority of the Persian king,
because Esther (later on) did the same thing in principle
without trouble. In fact she was able to obtain the king's
favour and save the Jews by breaking strict protocols.

Her words show that she too was well aware of the danger: 'All the king's officials and the people of the royal provinces know that for any man or woman who approaches the king in the inner court without being summoned the king has but one law: that he be put to death. The only exception to this is for the king to extend the gold sceptre to him and spare his life. But thirty days have passed since I was called to go to the king' (4:11). 'I will go to the king, even though it is against the law. And if I perish, I perish' (4:16). She was God's child acting in a godly way.

c. Irony of regret. We get a hint of irony at the start of the next chapter: 'Later when the anger of King Xerxes had subsided, he remembered Vashti and what she had done and what he had decreed about her.' This is a subtle indication that he may well have regretted banishing her. Certainly the full impact of his actions only dawned on him after he had calmed down. Maybe he realized that Vashti was not just a pretty face after all. Perhaps he recognized her strength of character in refusing his immature command. Act in haste, repent at leisure!

So the book of Esther is skilled human literature as well as being the very Word of God. It is an encouraging reminder that God's hand is no less powerful and no less active when not so obvious.

WHAT THE TEXT TEACHES

QUESTIONS FOR DISCUSSION

1. *Look up Exodus 20:1-17; Ephesians 5:22-23; and Colossians 3:18. How would each of the Ten Commandments clarify a wife's duty to submit to her husband 'as to the Lord' and 'as is fitting in the Lord'?*

2. *From a careful reading of the following verses, what is the Bible's teaching about alcohol? Genesis 9:21; 14:18; Exodus 29:40; Deuteronomy 14:26; Psalm 104:14-15; Proverbs 20:1; 23:29-30; Ecclesiastes 10:17; Isaiah 55:1; Luke 5:36-39; John 2:1-11; Ephesians 5:18; Romans 14:21; and 1 Timothy 5:23.*

CHAPTER THREE

TOMORROW'S PROBLEMS SOLVED TODAY

LOOK IT UP

BIBLE READING

Esther chapter 2

INTRODUCTION

We should understand the second chapter of this book in its covenant context: God is making sure that 'tomorrow's problems are solved today'. That is how it is with God. He is never confronted with spur-of-the-moment issues. He has always been at work ahead of time. He knows the end from the beginning. He knows what is around the corner and he is ready for it. He knows all the opposition that will come against the Messianic kingdom, but his wise plan already has the solutions in hand.

He carries out this plan by using the ordinary events of history. The events described in Esther 2 could just as well be found in any newspaper. It simply depicts life going on in the Persian Empire. True, it is a fairly sordid world of the rich and famous, but that's par for the course anywhere in the world at any point in history. Xerxes was typical of kings in the ancient Near East: they indulged in immorality, materialism and lavish party life. They had harems, which were just flesh-pots to satisfy their lusts. The first chapter has already introduced us to life in the Persian palace: a world of intrigue, deceptive diplomacy, piques of passion, and the drunken paranoia that decrees hasty and unenforceable laws. So why does chapter 2 continue to tell us what appears to be 'more of the same'? Why this lengthy narrative about the parade of beautiful women to select a new queen? Why the report on an item of local crime (the conspiracy that was foiled)?

The reason is that, quite apart from what men are doing, God is at work too. The writer shows us how God is preparing solutions today for tomorrow's problems. The reader isn't aware of a problem yet, nor are God's people who were there at the time. The problem is not revealed until the next chapter. We will soon meet the evil man Haman who is intent on annihilating every Jew. We will see him obtain royal permission to do so. But God is already preparing the solution before the problem arises. God arranges for two key people to be placed in positions of influence so he can use them to save the Jews from genocide. It is truly a case of 'tomorrow's problems being solved today'. The story revolves around two main events:

1. A queen crowned
2. A conspiracy found

WHAT THE TEXT TEACHES

A queen crowned

The political scene

Xerxes has had time to soberly calm down after banishing Vashti, and it is clear that he has some regrets. When a man acts in a state of drunkenness (as Xerxes did), and when his advisers are sycophantic diplomats (as they were), and when impractical laws are hastily imposed, a king is bound to wish he could turn the clock back. His memory is bound to haunt him. So 'Later when the anger of King Xerxes had subsided, he remembered Vashti and what she had done and what he had decreed about her' (2:1). Maybe the king's personal aides thought they would feel the brunt of his mood, so their initiative to cure him was to suggest searching for a new queen; and this pleased Xerxes. So the scene is set in the bizarre political situation of the Persian court.

The historical scene

The writer now provides us with a flashback to the year 597 B. C. (114 years earlier), when the Jews were deported from Jerusalem to Babylon for seventy years of exile. This is necessary in order to introduce the two key people in the rest of the story, Mordecai and Esther.

Mordecai is introduced first. From the tribe of Benjamin he also appears to be part of the royal family of Saul, Israel's first king. Mordecai descends from Kish who is Saul's ancestor (1 Samuel 9:1; 14:51; 1 Chronicles 8:33), and Shimei whose loyalty to Saul as his relative was so fierce that he cursed David (2 Samuel 16:5). Be careful how you understand verse 6: 'who had been carried into exile from Jerusalem by Nebuchadnezzar king of Babylon, among those taken captive with Jehoiachin king of Judah'. The 'who' refers to Mordecai, but was he among the exiles? Yes, but not in the literal and physical sense in 597 B. C. That would make both he and Esther too old in this present story in 483 B. C. It is an example of 'telescoping generations', treating families as a solidarity. Though he was yet unborn, Mordecai was 'carried into exile' in the loins of his family. That is why it is no simple task to try and estimate the age of the earth by counting back through the genealogies provided in the Old Testament. Formulae such as 'X begat Y' or 'P was the father of Q' are sometimes not chronological but telescopic. Generations are selectively skipped according to the purposes of the writer.

REMEMBER THIS

By telescoping generations, the Bible can talk about someone acting before they were born. So, 'One might even say that Levi, who collects the tenth, paid the tenth through Abraham, because

REMEMBER THIS

when Melchizedek met Abraham, Levi was still in the body of his ancestor' (Hebrews 7:9-10). Telescoping generations is just one example of how the Bible treats men in corporate solidarity. The gospel must be understood that way. 'In Adam all die, so in Christ all will be made alive' (1 Corinthians 15:22). When Adam sinned, all generations of his people were in solidarity with him (telescoped together). When Christ obeyed, all generations of his people were in solidarity with him (telescoped together). His righteousness becomes ours.

Esther was Mordecai's cousin. Her parents had died while she was a little girl so Mordecai had raised her as his own adopted daughter. The reader already suspects that she will do well in the beauty parade because: 'This girl ... was lovely in form and features.' But she wasn't just a pretty face. There was something about her that indicated mature character and wisdom. For a start, Hegai was immediately impressed with her. He had seen plenty of pretty girls, indeed, as keeper of the harem he spent his whole life surrounded by them. And it wasn't mainly physical attraction (the girls were safe with Hegai since he was a eunuch). 'Immediately he provided her with beauty treatments and special food. He assigned to her seven maids selected from the king's palace and moved her and her maids into the best place in the harem.'

There is also her respect for Mordecai, which comes out repeatedly in the story. Here we are told 'Esther had not revealed her nationality and family background, because Mordecai had forbidden her to do so' (v. 10). Though she has received much criticism from some readers ever since, the fact is that she was wise not to reveal her Jewish background. It is integral to what follows. The Lord God is using her beauty and secret identity as important factors in solving a looming crisis.

Esther's wisdom is also shown when her turn came to meet the king. The custom for girls in the harem was that 'Anything she wanted was given to her to take with her from the harem to the king's palace' (v. 13). This is the equivalent of being let loose in a big shopping centre with freedom to spend as much as you like on your choice of clothing, jewellery and hair-do, knowing that the palace will pay the bill. So what did Esther do? 'When the turn came for Esther ... to go to the king, she asked for nothing other than what Hegai ... suggested. And Esther won the favour of everyone who saw her' (v. 15). She had the sense to seek guidance from the man who knew best. She wore what was appropriate. No doubt her natural beauty was more obvious, being unspoiled by gaudy and excessive adornments.

WHAT THE TEXT TEACHES

The harem scene

We should not fail to see the awful reality of the harem. Behind all the visible beauty and perfume and the lavish palace life of indulgence for the girls, a harem was a place where the inhumanity of polygamy was experienced. Once in the harem, a girl was the king's property. If she was 'successful' (meaning she was called to spend a night with the king as his sex-object) she was automatically his polygamous wife (concubine) and the next morning she would 'return to another part of the harem to the care of Shaashgaz, the king's eunuch, who was in charge of the concubines. She would not return to the king unless he was pleased with her and summoned her by name' (v. 14). For many it was not likely the king would ever call her again. Why would he, since he had a large supply of beautiful virgins he has never met before. So they virtually became instant widows. In any case they never had a normal, loving, married relationship. They could not leave to marry the man they chose. It was emotional deprivation. It is a sad picture of moral degradation, and exploitative, lustful gratification for the kings of the ancient Near East, which trapped even Solomon, and became his undoing.

So, with those different scenarios in mind, Esther was crowned Queen of Persia; a great banquet was held in her honour and a holiday declared. God was ever active behind the scenes.

A conspiracy found

Mordecai has already been appointed as a Persian magistrate. That is what is meant by the phrase 'sitting at the king's gate' (v. 19). This expression occurs five times in this book. Throughout the ancient Near East 'the gate' was the place where justice was dispensed. It was not just a 'gate' as we know it, not just a gap in the wall, but a fairly substantial and often fortified area. This particular gate seems to have been close to the king's own room. The magistrate sat while the litigants stood pleading their case. We are not told how and when Mordecai was made a magistrate. One possibility is that Esther had arranged it upon becoming queen.

So Mordecai is in a good position to hear what palace officials were saying. One day he found out about a plot to assassinate[1] King Xerxes. He advised Esther, who in turn told the king. An official investigation found the two traitors behind it and they were hanged. These details were all recorded in the official annals of Persia in the king's presence. The only oversight was that Mordecai was not rewarded for his good detective work. This becomes a critical detail in chapter 6 when Xerxes, unable to sleep one night, was reading the official annals and realized Mordecai had not been rewarded. The way this unfolds shows how God has been working all these minor details to save the Jews. So this little crime report at the end of chapter 2 is vital. The Persian king now owes his life to a loyal Jew. God will use this so that the Jews will keep their lives.

Conclusion

Let us be greatly encouraged at the way our God 'causes all things to work together for the good' of his covenant people. Let us never interpret history simply in terms of what we can see humans doing. Behind it all is the unseen hand of almighty God making all things subservient to the kingdom of Christ. Who would have guessed that the banishment of Queen Vashti was one of the steps in God's provision for the Jews? God is always going ahead of his people. Their future is safely in his hands today. Tomorrow's problems for them have solutions in line today. God has been providing answers to tomorrow's prayers long before we even call on him. 'Your Father knows what you need before you ask him' (Matthew 6:8).

In his famous prophecy about the new heavens and new earth, Isaiah shows how good it will be for God's people. God says, 'Before they call I will answer' (Isaiah 65:24). That is true in principle even now! The book of Esther shows

God answering before they call. The covenant grace of
God in history means that the principles of the 'end
time' have intruded into our present time. Belonging
to God means we have a taste of heaven before we get
there. The blessings of the new earth are already felt in
the old earth. All praise to God.

QUESTIONS FOR DISCUSSION

1. *If God is at work in history using everyday events to
   achieve his plans, does that mean humans are not acting freely? Were the people in this story acting freely?
   See Matthew 17:12; Acts 2:22-24; and James 1:13-14.*

2. *How does the gospel itself indicate that God has gone
   ahead of us, solving our biggest problem? See
   Ephesians 1:3-8; Romans 5:6-8; and 1 Peter 1:1-2.*

CHAPTER FOUR

HAMAN THE HORRIBLE

LOOK IT UP

BIBLE READING

Esther 3

INTRODUCTION

History has thrown up some despicable characters and the one we meet here in Esther 3 is no exception: 'Haman son of Hammedatha, the Agagite', or as verse 10 ominously adds, 'Haman ... the enemy of the Jews'. For reasons unknown, he was appointed as prime minister, the highest position in the empire, answering only to King Xerxes. As Haman strutted about the empire, people were supposed to bow down to him. The king had especially commanded it. That would not normally be necessary because it was accepted protocol, and common courtesy, for high-ranking officials to be greeted with a bow of the head or knee. Most likely, Haman was already known as an unpleasant character. People would not have bowed to him unless required to do so by law.

However, one good man refused: Mordecai the Jew. Readers already know him as the hero who saved the king's life. Haman, deeply resenting Mordecai's refusal to bow, resolved to murder every single Jew in the empire. He was prepared to spill so much blood in revenge for a personal rebuff.

Yet not even this story of 'Haman the horrible' is recorded for us for moral reasons. The author is not giving Haman the bad publicity he deserves in order to draw out our derision and renew our resolve to be better people. The setting for the whole Bible is covenantal. Again, we are to see how God is at work in all the details and intrigues of human history, ruling and overruling so that all opposition to his covenant fails, and his promise to send a Saviour, 'the seed of the woman', will be fulfilled.

THINK ABOUT IT

Biblical revelation is organic, meaning it grows and progresses in clarity. So the first gospel promise in Genesis 3:15 does not reveal the many details that only become clear later. All it tells us is that a male descended from Adam and Eve will destroy the serpent, but it will cost him injury (a bruised heel). As revelation continues, we see this 'seed of the woman' progressively defined as the 'seed of Abraham', descendant of David, and Son of God. We also learn progressively that his 'bruising' means his sacrificial death to atone for the sins of his people (Isaiah 53). The outworking of Genesis 3:15 is found in Jesus Christ at Calvary.

A moralistic agenda has caused many readers to entirely miss the point of this book. With regard to this third chapter, heavy weather is made of one issue in particular: Shouldn't Mordecai have obeyed the governing authority by bowing to Haman? Isn't his civil disobedience the cause of all the trouble? Surprisingly, Mordecai's refusal has been described as 'stubborn', 'persistent obstinacy' and 'pig-headed' even by otherwise reliable writers.[1] Another writer moralizes Mordecai's grief when he 'tore his clothes, put on sackcloth and ashes, and went out into the city, wailing loudly and bitterly' (4:1), saying that it was then too late: he should have thought about the cost of his actions beforehand. So the moral drawn is 'look before you leap'.

That is not how the inspired New Testament writers approach the Old Testament. They look at events in terms of their connection with 'salvation-history'. In other words, they are always drawing lines from the Old Testament events to the Christ-events. Lines that begin in the shadows converge in the full light of Christ. We can grasp the covenant framework here by dealing with two questions about the villain in this chapter, 'Haman the horrible':

1. Why was he horrible?
2. How was he horrible?

Why was he horrible?

Of course the superficial answer lies in Mordecai's refusal to bow to him: 'When Haman saw that Mordecai
would not kneel down or pay him honour, he was enraged. Yet having learned who Mordecai's people were,
he scorned the idea of killing only Mordecai. Instead
Haman looked for a way to destroy all Mordecai's
people, the Jews, throughout the whole kingdom of
Xerxes' (vv. 5-6). But there is a much bigger agenda here:
we need to understand *why* Mordecai refused to bow.
It was not simply a personal insult. To take that line is
to trivialize the whole issue. Nor was it merely a cultural problem, as if Jews did not bow to anyone. The
Old Testament proves that the custom of bowing down
before an important person was common in Israel too,
as in the ancient Near East generally (see 2 Samuel 14:4;
18:28; 1 Kings 1:16).

Nor was it due to a defect in Mordecai's character.
His daily associates and the officials he mixed with
saw no defect: 'Then the royal officials at the king's
gate asked Mordecai, "Why do you disobey the king's
command?" Day after day they spoke to him but he
refused to comply. Therefore they told Haman about it
to see whether Mordecai's behaviour would be tolerated, for he had told them he was a Jew' (vv 3-4). They
could not understand why this honourable man who
served as a magistrate observing proper protocols every
day would 'buck the system' in this one case. His loyalty
to Persia and its king were unquestioned. This is no

rebel. But the only answer he gave them was that he was a Jew.

Another important clue is given in verse 6: 'Yet having learned who Mordecai's people were, he scorned the idea of killing only Mordecai. Instead Haman looked for a way to destroy all Mordecai's people, the Jews, throughout the whole kingdom of Xerxes.' Haman is anti-Semitic in a major way! He is presented as an inveterate enemy of the Jews. He doesn't just hate the one Jew who injured his inflated ego: he hates all Jews everywhere! We have already seen this in verse 10. The point is that whatever Mordecai did or did not do, he was a Jew, and that is all that mattered to Haman. He hated the covenant people of God. There is a fanatical religious issue behind it all. This man Haman loathes the church of God in its Old Testament form. So this should alert us and cause us to ask: 'What is the big picture here?' What picture does the Old Testament paint of Haman the Agagite? What is the covenant setting for this Mordecai versus Haman polemic, this 'Jew' versus 'Jew hater'?

The biblical picture

When the author tells us Haman is an *Agagite,* it is a loaded statement. Agag was king of the Amalekites, the descendants of Amalek. Amalek is the grandson of Esau (1 Chronicles 1:34-36). The enmity between Jacob and Esau was proverbial. Esau's descendants are traditional enemies of Israel (Jacob's descendants). A key text here is Exodus 17. The children of Israel were at a place called Rephidim on their journey to the promised land. There the Amalekites attacked them. As Moses held up his arms, Joshua led the army against Amalek. God not only gave Israel the victory but a solemn assurance also:

> Then the LORD said to Moses, 'Write this on a scroll as something to be remembered and make sure that Joshua hears it, because I will completely blot out the memory of Amalek from under heaven.' Moses built an altar and called it The LORD is my Banner. He said, 'For hands were lifted up to the throne of the LORD. The LORD will be at war against the Amalekites from generation to generation' (Exodus 17:14-16).

So the issue here is 'pan-historical'. God is opposed to every generation of Amalekites, and Mordecai's refusal to honour Haman has to be seen in that context. It is not simply an isolated event in 483 B. C. It is thoroughly covenantal. His refusal to honour the Amalekite (Haman) is an indication that Mordecai knows the Word of God and has aligned himself with Jehovah. But many Israelites softened their stance, ignoring God's covenant oath. Many were prone to forget their enemies, they made peace with the devil, and the cost was always terrible. So when the forty years of wandering ended, and Israel was about to enter the promised land, it is not surprising that God renewed his warnings about Amalek:

> Remember what the Amalekites did to you along the way when you came out of Egypt. When you were weary and worn out, they met you on your journey and cut off all who were lagging behind; they had no fear of God. When the LORD your God gives you rest from all the enemies around you in the land he is giving you to possess as an inheritance, you shall blot out the memory of Amalek from under heaven. Do not forget! (Deuteronomy 25:17-19).

But they did forget. Their first king, Saul, was told by God, 'This is what the LORD Almighty says: "I will punish the Amalekites for what they did to Israel when they waylaid them as they came up from Egypt. Now go, attack the Amalekites and totally destroy everything that belongs to them. Do not spare them; put to death men and women, children and infants, cattle and sheep, camels and donkeys"' (1 Samuel 15:2-3). But Saul disobeyed and God rejected him as king from that moment. Saul foolishly left Agag the Amalekite king alive. It was left to Samuel to carry out God's Word, destroying Agag at Gilgal.

WHAT THE TEXT TEACHES

So what we have in Persia in 483 B. C. is a historic repeat of exactly the same agenda, Israel versus Amalek, Saul versus Agag. Here is Mordecai, the Jewish descendant of Saul (see 2:5). And here is Haman, the Amalekite descendant of Agag. Will Mordecai make the same mistake as Saul? Will he spare the inveterate enemy of God and refuse to impose the covenant ban on him? No, Mordecai stood firm. While it was not his place to kill the Amalekite (as it was with Saul and Joshua and Samuel), Mordecai showed great courage in refusing to bow to Haman. As a magistrate he knew full well the cost of disobeying the command of a Persian king. He was obviously prepared to suffer that, to put his own life on the line, rather than go against God. We can now see how far off-course the moralistic approach is. To condemn Mordecai as 'pig-headed', a civil-disobedient whose actions brought his whole Jewish population to the brink of extermination, is to misunderstand the situation completely.

REMEMBER THIS

We have just seen an example of how each part of Scripture has to be interpreted in harmony with the whole. This is sometimes called the 'analogy of Scripture' or 'the hermeneutical circle'. The 'small picture' (e.g. Amalek in Esther 3) has to be informed by the 'big picture' (Amalek in the rest of Scripture). Reliable biblical interpretation always observes that principle.

For those who insist on asking whether Mordecai was right in refusing to honour Haman, the reply is, yes, he was right. He was theologically astute. He understood the biblical ethic of giving 'honour to whom honour is due' and God has made it very plain that honour is not due to Amalek. Mordecai followed exactly the same ethic as the Apostles. He knew that a man's duty to obey the governing authorities has limits. We are obliged to obey rulers in all areas of their God-given mandate; but once they impose laws that clash with the authority of God, laws that force us to compromise our loyalty to God, then human government has to be disobeyed (Acts 4:19). Xerxes' command that men should honour Haman the Amalekite by bowing to him created an ethical dilemma for Jews. It was contrary to God's covenant oath. Maybe Xerxes the Gentile did not know that, but Mordecai the devout Jew did. So Mordecai was morally bound to refuse Haman.

The ultimate picture

Can you see where these lines finally converge? Can you see the ultimate stand-off between the covenant man of God and the inveterate enemy? Can you see the ultimate leader of Israel and the ultimate Amalek? Can you recall that most faithful Israelite who stood before the most powerful enemy of God in the entire world and was expected to bow the knee? It was Jesus in his wilderness temptations. As with Mordecai, the bowing could have been justified as mere protocol. So long as Jesus bowed in mere recognition of satanic power, who cares what attitude is in his heart? Just as Mordecai could have loathed Haman, Jesus would have loathed Satan, but the mere outward act is all that was expected. The stakes were high. The cost of refusal was a lot of misery for all Haman's people and all Christ's people. But refusal it must be, because the issue is essentially religious. It is essentially covenantal. It is essentially the point where inferior authority clashes head on with God's authority. It is really a question of 'Who shall be God?' So Jesus puts the ultimate issue on record as he, like Mordecai, refused to bow the knee: 'It is written: "Worship the Lord your God and serve him only"' (Luke 4:8). God alone shall determine my actions, God speaking in his covenant word.

How was he horrible?

Given that we have just identified Haman as essentially satanic, it is not surprising that his behaviour shows qualities typical of that. Notice in particular the hatred, the superstition and the lies.

Haman's hatred

What a despicably evil heart is revealed in verse 6: 'Having learned who Mordecai's people were, he scorned the idea of killing only Mordecai. Instead Haman looked for a way to destroy all Mordecai's people, the Jews, throughout the whole kingdom of Xerxes.' Even the idea of murdering one man was seen as totally inadequate revenge for his injured pride: 'he scorned the idea'. Instead, he insisted on the total annihilation of every Jew in Persia. Hatred has run over its banks! He is not content to kill one Jew or ten Jews or a thousand Jews or most Jews or all Jews except two or three. Nothing less than complete genocide is demanded by this fanatical hater of Jehovah. We see here a biblical theme that is found also in evil men like Lamech ('If Cain is avenged seven times, then Lamech seventy-seven times' — Genesis 4:24), and Herod (who was willing to kill all baby boys in order to get one), and ultimately Satan himself who 'prowls around like a roaring lion looking for someone to devour' (1 Peter 5:8).

As further evidence, look at the horrific terms of Haman's edict: 'to destroy, kill and annihilate all the Jews — young and old, women and little children — on a single day ... and to plunder their goods' (v. 13). Haman intends to cause maximum trauma. There is no trace of common decency. Then to complete the ghastly scene, the chapter closes with his abysmal human indifference: 'The king and Haman sat down to drink, but the city of Susa was bewildered' (v. 15). Here is corruption in high places.

Haman's superstition

A common characteristic of godlessness is superstition, occultic interests, any notion that human history is determined by 'fate', 'luck' or 'stars' rather than almighty God. Satan loves people to be guided by witches and mediums and spirits and stars and planets and dice and anything else, as long as it isn't the Word of God. So, 'In the first month, the month of Nisan, they cast the *pur* (that is, the lot) in the presence of Haman to select a day and month. And the lot fell on the twelfth month, the month of Adar' (v. 7). The fact that this occurred on the first month is not a coincidence. Persians believed that the 'gods' assembled together in the first month of each year to fix the 'fates' of men. So casting the lot was their way of finding out the 'luckiest' day. No Persian wanted to 'tempt fate' by failing to consult the numbers. Haman's day was the thirteenth day of the last month. So that is the day he chose to kill the Jews, that is the day that superstition decreed was *best* for success, which is ironic, for that was the *worst* decision he ever made, and it led to his death. The man exalted to the highest place was soon hanging on the highest gallows. The solemn truth is stated in Proverbs 16:33 and 16:4: 'The lot is cast into the lap, but its every decision is from the Lord'; 'The Lord works out everything for his own ends — even the wicked for a day of disaster.'

WHAT THE TEXT TEACHES

Haman's lies

Satan, 'the father of lies', is expert at mixing truth with falsehood, making a cocktail that seems to be in your best interests. Haman shows this family likeness as he appeals to Xerxes' advantage. 'Haman said to King Xerxes, "There is a certain people dispersed and scattered among the peoples in all the provinces of your kingdom whose customs are different from those of all other people and who do not obey the king's laws; it is not in the king's best interest to tolerate them. If it pleases the king, let a decree be issued to destroy them, and I will put ten thousand talents of silver into the royal treasury for the men who carry out this business"' (vv. 8-9).

This is very deceitful. Nowhere does he mention his real reason (the refusal of just one Jew to honour him). There was no evidence that the Jews were rebellious to Persian rule. All the evidence shows that they were industrious and law-abiding. And there was bribery: 10,000 talents of silver (345 metric tons). The king was quite disinterested in the whole matter: 'Keep the money ... and do with the people as you please' (v. 11). So Haman the horrible nursed his hatred for eleven months, looking forward to his day of slaughter.

Conclusion

The principle here is that human history, even in its darkest times, is simply a sub-set of covenant history. God is working behind the scenes to secure the ultimate welfare of his chosen people. He makes good use of them as his loyal servants (like Esther and Mordecai), he makes good use of even foolish kings like Xerxes, and, unlikely as it appears to us, he makes use of even despicable men like Haman (Proverbs 16:4). God has a covenant purpose in Christ and it will succeed fully and perfectly and eternally. Every weapon lifted against it is doomed to fail. All resistance will fail. 'Christ shall have dominion over land and sea, earth's remotest regions shall His empire be'.[2]

It is not just Scripture that we must interpret covenantally, but history, our modern history, all history. Sometimes things look bleak for the church of God. In addition to the unseen enemies attacking like a virus from within, there are the 'Hamans' who rise up with power in their hands. While it is right for God's people to stand firm and resist, it is not right to adopt a pessimistic outlook. God is still in control. There is no case for paranoia and a defeatist mentality. They were dark days for the dispersed Old Testament church in 400 B.C. They had a terrible enemy about to devour them. But behind the scenes they had a great deliverer ready to defend them. 'The one who is in you is greater than the one who is in the world' (1 John 4:4). We must never forget it.

DISCUSS IT

QUESTIONS FOR DISCUSSION

1. Why can't wickedness finally triumph? See Acts 2:23-24; Romans 8:38-39.

2. Why is superstition foolish? See Psalm 135:6; Proverbs 16:9,33; Isaiah 46:9-11; Daniel 4:34-35; Ephesians 1:11.

3. Why is pessimism unwarranted for believers? See 1 Chronicles 29:10-12; Isaiah 14:24,27; 1 Peter 1:3-4.

CHAPTER FIVE

'IF I PERISH, I PERISH'

BIBLE READING

Esther 4

With the words 'If I perish, I perish', Esther resolved a personal crisis in her own life as well as a crisis for her Jewish nation. It was a crisis of faith, a crisis of loyalty, a crisis with major consequences. From inside the palace she kept in touch with Mordecai outside by using a trusted mediator named Hathach. The courage of her critical decision is proved by a commendable mixture of human qualities: her humility, intelligence, caution and proper fear. Fully aware of the risks, she resolved to lay her life on the line. 'I will go to the king, even though it is against the law. And if I perish, I perish' (v. 16).

This was a religious act. Esther has deliberately chosen to publicly align herself with God's covenant people in their dark hour. She has spoken like Joshua of old: 'As for me and my house, we will serve Jehovah.' This is a major point in the book: in fact it is a turning point in covenant history. And it serves to remind us that the faithful decisions of God's people anywhere may be far more significant than they could ever have anticipated. It will serve us well to understand this part of Scripture. Why? Because the demands of loyalty to God might bring us to a crisis also, where we have to act against human laws and protocols. We can profit from this text by considering:

1. The actual crisis
2. The authentic courage
3. The appropriate lessons

The actual crisis

The crisis in general

The crisis facing Esther arose because Mordecai had refused to bow to Haman even though the king had commanded it. As we have seen, this was not a petty or perverse refusal. It was not due to stubbornness or any other character defect in Mordecai. It was a decision of faith, an indication of his loyalty to God and his covenant oath. Haman's intense anti-Semitism, his intention to wipe out every Jew, shows that his Amalekite nature is not just skin deep. We must not imagine for one moment that the Amalekite religion had improved with age.

So Mordecai aligned himself with God, refusing to forget the covenant. It was a courageous act because, being a magistrate, he knew the cost of disobeying the command of a Persian king. Haman reacted by deceiving the king into authorizing the mass murder of every Jew in Persia. The decree was published throughout the empire. This dreadful news was devastating to the Jews. Even ordinary Persians in the capital city were aghast, in contrast to the callous indifference of their leaders: 'The king and Haman sat down to drink, but the city of Susa was bewildered' (3:15). The author tells us of the impact on the Jews:

When Mordecai learned of all that had been done, he tore his clothes, put on sackcloth and ashes, and went out into the city, wailing loudly and bitterly. But he went only as far as the king's gate, because no one clothed in sackcloth was allowed to enter it. In every province to which the edict and order of the king came, there was great mourning among the Jews, with fasting, weeping and wailing. Many lay in sackcloth and ashes (4:1-3).

It seems that members of the harem and others living in the confines of the palace were somewhat sheltered from day-to-day events outside, because it took some time for Esther to hear about the crisis. But eventually her maids informed her and 'she was in great distress' (4:4). She sent some clothes to Mordecai so he could come and see her, since sackcloth (an emblem of mourning) was not allowed in the palace. When he declined, Esther sent her personal representative, Hathach, to visit Mordecai. There was nothing private about the ensuing dialogue, since Hathach and Mordecai met in a very public place, 'in the open square of the city in front of the king's gate' (4:6). Mordecai was candid and detailed in describing the crisis and he sent Hathach back, urging Esther to stand up and be counted.

> Mordecai told him everything that had happened to him, including the exact amount of money Haman had promised to pay into the royal treasury for the destruction of the Jews. He also gave him a copy of the text of the edict for their annihilation, which had been published in Susa, to show to Esther and explain it to her, and he told him to urge her to go into the king's presence to beg for mercy and plead with him for her people (4:7-8).

The crisis in particular

That made the crisis very personal for Esther. She was 'between a rock and a hard place'. On the one hand, she dearly loved Mordecai, the cousin who had raised her as his daughter. His pain was her pain. And of course she felt the terrible anguish of all her fellow Jews. On the other hand, no one can just 'pop in' to visit the King of Persia, not even the queen. Top bureaucrats strictly arranged all visits to the king, Haman the prime minister being ultimately responsible. There was good reason for this. It gave the king protection from assassins and from the nuisance of common complaints and issues that should not bother the throne. To violate protocol here was to invite death. So Esther responded to Mordecai in the following terms: 'All the king's officials and the people of the royal provinces know that for any man or woman who approaches the king in the inner court without being summoned the king has but one law: that he be put to death. The only exception to this is for the king to extend the gold sceptre to him and spare his life. But thirty days have passed since I was called to go to the king' (4:11).

The crisis develops

Mordecai's response is one of those brilliantly apt and weighty speeches that moves people, inspiring heroic action, clarifying the course of duty, and from the human perspective, changing the course of history. Listen to his words: 'Do not think that because you are in the king's house you alone of all the Jews will escape. For if you remain silent at this time, relief and deliverance for the Jews will arise from another place, but you and your father's family will perish. And who knows but that you have come to royal position for such a time as this?' (4:12-14). Notice his three main points:

1. Face the reality! This is a candid wake-up call because Esther obviously assumes that her own life is not in danger so long as she doesn't break palace protocols. She thinks she is immune from the death threat in Haman's decree. So Mordecai tells her the truth. The reality is that there are no loopholes in the coming annihilation. Every Jew is on death row. There will be no exceptions. The edict is terrible in its thoroughness, 'to destroy, kill and annihilate all the Jews — young and old, women and little children — on a single day'. Don't deceive yourself that it means all Jews except Esther! The laws of the Medes and Persians are set in concrete. There was no escape clause for the previous queen, Vashti, even though the law she broke wasn't even made until after the event. So what hope does Esther have in breaking a law already in force?

2. Don't sit on the fence! Esther has to make a choice so Mordecai tells her, 'If you remain silent at this time, relief and deliverance for the Jews will arise from another place.' How can he be so confident? Because he knows that God will stick to his oath. God has sworn that he will be at war with Amalek in every generation. God will blot out Amalek from under heaven. He will not let Amalek (Haman) blot out Israel. Mordecai is a man of faith, utterly convinced that God's word is truth. So he knows that God will deliver the Jews from this present crisis, otherwise God has spoken falsely. God can use Esther, but he does not depend on her or anyone else. If she remains silent, only she will lose. God can raise up children for Abraham out of the very stones. So what will it be, Esther? Are you willing for God to deliver Israel through your faithfulness, or through someone else? Make up your mind.

3. *Seize the moment!* Look at the providential opportunities before you! 'Who knows but that you have come to royal position for such a time as this?' 'Do you think it is merely coincidental that you, a Jew, became queen at the very time when Jews need help? Do you think it merely coincidental that your husband, the king, owes his life to a Jew, to me, your cousin?' In other words Mordecai suggests that she stops looking only on the negative side. She must stop considering only the risks involved. Esther needs to recognize the very real advantages she has. In God's providence Esther is better placed than anyone on earth to meet the need of the moment.

The authentic courage

There is a difference between brashness and true courage. Brash people are foolhardy. They trifle with risks and dangers, making light of them. There is haughtiness in the steps of the foolhardy, a lack of perspective, and a surreal air about them. But we see none of that in Esther. Authentic courage is well aware of the risks, faces up to reality, and fears true danger, but it pushes on anyway because it is driven by motives even weightier than personal safety. Notice Esther's character in this critical hour.

She was teachable. As an intelligent person, Esther felt the impact of Mordecai's stirring speech. Though her fears are still real she resolved to act bravely. Her subsequent actions prove her to be courageous, humble and godly. She was willing to be seen taking correction from Mordecai, and she asked for help. She needed God's help so she said: 'Go, gather together all the Jews who are in Susa, and fast for me. Do not eat or drink for three days, night or day. I and my maids will fast as you do. When this is done, I will go to the king, even though it is against the law. And if I perish, I perish.'

REMEMBER THIS

Though there is a divine sanctity to human life, it is not without limits. Self-denial sometimes requires a willingness to lay down our life. It is the highest expression of love: 'Greater love has no one than this, that he lay down his life for his friends' (John 15:13). Esther was prepared to do it. But human words are inadequate to describe Christ's love, for he laid down his life not for friends, but enemies (Romans 5:8,10).

Though prayer is not explicitly mentioned, it nearly always went with Jewish fasting. Fasting was usually only for one day. It was obligatory for the Day of Atonement (Leviticus 16:29-31) but otherwise it was a voluntary matter. The fact that her own maids joined the fast is significant. Few if any would be Jews. But there was a good rapport of love and trust. Remember, 'Esther won the favour of everyone who saw her' (2:15). So now they would all know that she was a Jew grieving along with all the Jews in Persia. Essentially, Esther agrees with the hymn written two millennia later by Isaac Watts:

I'm not ashamed to own my Lord,
Or to defend His cause,
Maintain the glory of His Cross,
And honour all His laws.[1]

She has accepted Mordecai's challenge, expressed in a hymn by Norman O. Formes:

Rise up, you saints of God,
His Kingdom's task embrace!
Redress sin's cruel consequence;
Give justice greater place.[2]

So there we see God working his covenant purposes out, blessing the wise and faithful efforts of his people (though clothed in weakness, fear and trembling), and cursing the wicked efforts of his enemies (clothed in power and arrogance). What practical lessons can we legitimately learn from all this?

The appropriate lessons

1. Regarding guidance from providence

Be wary of the common tendency to treat God's providential ordering of events in our lives as 'guidance'. Do not assume they are pointers to what he expects us to do. In other words, we must not extrapolate from Esther's case to our case. Esther is not 'every Christian'. Her case is unique. It is not typical of our situation. The fact that God had providentially made her queen in Persia *was* a major factor in her decision-making, but that does not mean providence should have such a grip on our decision-making.

It may be tempting to appeal to Mordecai's words to Esther: 'Who knows but that you have come to royal position for such a time as this?' Isn't he appealing to providence as an indication of the will of God for her? No, not if this is all he said. 'Who knows?' is a valid question to ask of providence generally. But that is not all he said. He has just made a major statement: 'If you remain silent at this time, relief and deliverance for the Jews will arise from another place.' This throws more light on his question 'Who knows?' This puts more pressure on Esther than a mere open-ended question. It implies that God's will for Esther is for her to speak up. It implies that she will be failing her duty by remaining silent, and will forfeit some blessings as a result. It is hard to escape the conclusion that Mordecai is using providence as a lever. In reality he is answering his own question. In effect he is saying: 'God has made you Queen of Persia so you could meet the needs of this hour in delivering the Jews. Your silence would be very inappropriate.' Who knows? Mordecai knows, and so does Esther now.

I must repeat, however, that this case is unique. Why? Because God *has* spoken directly to the essential issue confronting Esther, namely the issue of Amalekite opposition to Israel. God has promised to be at war against Amalek in every generation. God will not let Amalek destroy his covenant people. He will blot out the memory of Amalek from under heaven. So Mordecai knows that there is more than providential guidance here. He has the direct guidance of Scripture. God will deliver Israel, and if Esther refuses to stand up, it will be to her loss; but God will still deliver Israel.

However, we cannot argue like that. God has not explicitly spoken on the numerous decisions we need to make in daily life. Appeals based on providence can be very manipulative 'guilt trips', even unconsciously. Mordecai's appeal was not a guilt trip for Esther. *We cannot say* to someone in the church, 'We need a teacher for a Bible class, a Sunday-school class, and in the providence of God you are a trained teacher, so that's God's will for you.' We cannot say, 'If you refuse then you will suffer loss for it.' That is presumption. In other words, we should not regard providence as 'the leading of God'.

Providence is generally ambiguous. For example, if in God's providence a man has evident academic and teaching gifts, he is left with numerous options. He could do well as a preacher, a university lecturer, a barrister, a minister of state, an author, or many other careers. He is free to make his choice. No one can presume to see 'God's leading' in any one direction. *Providence is not revelation*. True guidance lies in making decisions that are consistent with Scripture. That leaves us a great deal of freedom. Yes, providence should always be considered. If you are not good at maths then do not set your heart on being a rocket scientist. That is not consistent with the wisdom commended in Scripture. But mathematical skill is not a clue that God wants you to be a rocket scientist. Let each person weigh up his opportunities in the light of his God-given abilities and make good biblical decisions. Let us abandon all mystical talk about 'God's leading', as if God is dropping little hints to guide us. *Sola Scriptura!*

2. Regarding civil disobedience

When Esther said, 'I will go to the king, even though it is against the law', she was touching the same problem of conscience that faces all believers. Somewhere, sometime, religious principle will clash with human law and protocol. To be loyal to God, civil disobedience is the only faithful option. We will have to defy human conventions, laws and expectations. That is why Mordecai refused to honour Haman. That is why Esther decided to break the Persian law. That is why the Apostles defied the Roman command to stop preaching the gospel (Acts 4). But, civil disobedience should never be done lightly, boastfully, disdainfully, or provocatively. On the contrary, it should be done with respect, humility and prayer. Courage will be needed to accept any penalty that could arise as a consequence. So Esther said, 'If I perish, I perish.' Likewise, the Apostles patiently endured chains as model prisoners. So also Christ subjected himself to injustice, even crucifixion. Christians should not flaunt their spiritual loyalty to Christ, nor should we compromise it. 'Give to Caesar the things that are Caesar's, and to God the things that are God's.'

3. Regarding fasting

It is sometimes asked whether Christians should practise fasting today? The question arises naturally because Esther called a fast to seek God's blessing. Fasting was also used at various points in Israel's history as a way for believers to humble themselves before God and to focus on prayer. For example, Ezra 8:21-23 says, 'I proclaimed a fast, so that we might humble

ourselves before our God and ask him for a safe journey for us and our children, with all our possessions...
So we fasted and petitioned our God about this, and he
answered our prayer.' The question of fasting was asked
directly to Jesus. Some people who were fasting (disciples of John the Baptist) noticed that other Christians
were not, so they said to Jesus: 'How is it that we and
the Pharisees fast, but your disciples do not fast?'
(Matthew 9:14). In other words, shouldn't Christians
practise fasting? For the answer (and the reasoning) see
Appendix A at the end of this book.

QUESTIONS FOR DISCUSSION

1. *According to Acts 4:16-20 and Acts 5:28-29, when does
   a Christian need to disobey the civil government?*

2. *Is civil government simply 'a necessary evil'? Read carefully Romans 13:1-7 and 1 Peter 2:11-23.*

3. *How does Acts 16:19-34 encourage us to remain godly
   even when persecuted by a non-Christian authority?*

4. *Though providence is not an infallible guide in decision-
   making, it is a useful factor to take into account. How
   do the examples in 1 Thessalonians 3:1-2 and
   Philippians 2:25-26 show that?*

5. *According to 2 Timothy 3:16-17, what is the role of Scripture in daily life?*

CHAPTER SIX

THE KING
AND I

BIBLE READING

Esther 5-6

INTRODUCTION

We are right in the middle of the book in chapters 5-6, and right at the turning point of the whole drama. The narrative here is structured around two 'king and I' scenes. Each is the opposite of the other. In the first, we see Esther's admirable qualities rewarded: her humility, her wisdom, her faith and her courage. In the second scene, we see the despicable qualities of Haman justly rewarded too. He sings his 'king and I' song in 5:12 as he boasts: 'I'm the only person Queen Esther invited to accompany the king to the banquet she gave. And she has invited me along with the king tomorrow.' But he got a lot more than he bargained for. His meeting with King Xerxes (6:6-10) was the beginning of the end for Haman.

The results of these two scenes are cleverly related by the author. The hand of God is very much at work in both, as he sovereignly rules over all. In the first case Esther is rewarded by grace and favour that is instrumental in saving God's covenant people from the decree of annihilation hanging over them. In the second case, the justice of God stabs away at Haman. The author heaps up irony upon irony. Through a number of little details, Haman becomes his own worst enemy. His own character defects ruin him. His advantages become his disadvantages. His 'king and I' song becomes his funeral dirge. The gallows he built for the murder of Mordecai becomes his own deathbed. The honour he presumed for himself went to Mordecai. He signed his own death warrant by begging mercy from Esther: when he fell down before her, it was seen from a distance by the king, who thought it was a sexual assault. That was the end of Haman.

The covenant theme that ties all this together is well stated in Isaiah 54:17, where God promised his people: 'No weapon forged against you will prevail.' The prophet's words a few verses earlier are well known: 'Though the mountains be shaken and the hills be removed, yet my unfailing love for you will not be shaken nor my covenant of peace be removed, says the LORD, who has compassion on you' (v. 10). These words apply to Israel at the very time God was chastising her. It was reassurance for the church even when God's rod of discipline was being felt, just as it was in the exile and Esther's situation in Persia.

Even when disciplining us God is being merciful. He assures the church in every age: 'If anyone does attack you, it will not be my doing; whoever attacks you will surrender to you. "See, it is I who created the blacksmith who fans the coals into flame and forges a weapon fit for its work. And it is I who have created the destroyer to work havoc; no weapon forged against you will prevail, and you will refute every tongue that accuses you. This is the heritage of the servants of the LORD, and this is their vindication from me," declares the LORD' (vv. 15-17). God is in complete control of every weapon raised against his church. He controls the manufacturer of the weapon (the blacksmith) and the hand that wields it (the destroyer who works havoc). Haman has weapons raised against God's people in Persia, intending to cause chaos against them. But he will fail because God is faithful. Let's take a look at these two 'king and I' scenes:

1. The king and Esther
2. The king and Haman

The king and Esther

On the third day Esther put on her royal robes and stood in the inner court of the palace, in front of the king's hall. The king was sitting on his royal throne in the hall, facing the entrance. When he saw Queen Esther standing in the court, he was pleased with her and held out to her the gold sceptre that was in his hand. So Esther approached and touched the tip of the sceptre. Then the king asked, 'What is it,

Queen Esther? What is your request? Even up to half the kingdom, it will be given you.' 'If it pleases the king,' replied Esther, 'let the king, together with Haman, come today to a banquet I have prepared for him.' 'Bring Haman at once,' the king said, 'so that we may do what Esther asks.' So the king and Haman went to the banquet Esther had prepared. As they were drinking wine, the king again asked Esther, 'Now what is your petition? It will be given you. And what is your request? Even up to half the kingdom, it will be granted.' Esther replied, 'My petition and my request is this: If the king regards me with favour and if it pleases the king to grant my petition and fulfil my request, let the king and Haman come tomorrow to the banquet I will prepare for them. Then I will answer the king's question' (5:1 8).

One of the important things to note here is that God's promise to defend his people does not detract from their responsibility to stand and fight. God's faithfulness is never a cue for our slackness. His provision of our daily bread goes hand in hand with our duty to work for it. His promise to break the weapons hurled against the gospel is no reason for us to merely sit back and watch the devastation. There must be a proper counter-attack. If God is involved in the polemic against evil, so are God's people. The faith that pleases God always goes hand in hand with responsible human activity.

Jesus said, 'If you love me, you will obey what I command' (John 14:15). Genuine trust is not passive but active. It is never just orthodox beliefs in the mind. Those beliefs are always evident in an obedient life. 'Faith by itself, if it is not accompanied by action, is dead' (James 2:17).

Consistent with this principle, Esther made her bold stand. As well as courage, she displays other good qualities.

Wisdom

Esther shows considerable wisdom. She had been fasting in the custom of the Jews, but she did not let it show. She looked her regal best before going to the king. She is the very opposite of the hypocrites whom Jesus later condemned: 'When you fast, do not look sombre as the hypocrites do, for they disfigure their faces to show men they are fasting... But when you fast, put oil on your head and wash your face, so that it will not be obvious to men that you are fasting, but only to your Father, who is unseen; and your Father, who sees what is done in secret, will reward you' (Matthew 6:16-18).

Her request for a private banquet is evidence of her wisdom. She senses that this is not the place to be making her requests known about such momentous things. This is the great court where the king sits to receive petitioners. His courtiers, advisers and guards surround him. A private dinner would be more suitable. It was both courageous and honourable to invite Haman along. Esther was going to accuse him to his face, not behind his back. But of course that gave Haman the opportunity to speak for himself and to lie his way out of trouble by exerting his influence as prime minister. He was, after all, the king's top man, his favourite and recently exalted official. So it is still a risky business.

Faith

Her faith is clear, not only by alignment with God and his people, but also by her having already prepared the banquet. 'Let the king, together with Haman, come today to a banquet I *have prepared* for him.' She left nothing to chance, doing what was humanly responsible, even though the outcome is in God's hands. We should understand the king's repeated words of generosity as purely cultural and idiomatic: 'What is your request? Even up to half the kingdom, it will be given you.' In today's language we might say: 'I'll give you the shirt off my back', or 'I'd give my right arm'. In other words, he tells Esther, 'Ask for what you desire, I'll do my utmost to help you.' The same expression is found in the grim context where Herod offered Salome up to half his kingdom, so she asked for John the Baptist's head (Mark 6:23).

The king and Haman

The fascinating thing in the story now is the writer's focus on three things that become important for the end results, namely, character defects, little details and irony.

Character defects

Haman's character defects are plain to see. There is his *ego*: 'I'm the only person Queen Esther invited to accompany the king to the banquet' (5:12). There is his *pride:* 'Haman boasted to them about his vast wealth, his many sons, and all the ways the king had honoured him and how he had elevated him above the other nobles and officials' (5:11). There is also his intense *hatred:* 'When he saw Mordecai at the king's gate and observed that he neither rose nor showed fear in his presence, he was filled with rage' (5:9). There is his *evil mind* which was only comforted by the prospect of murder: 'His wife Zeresh and all his friends said to him, "Have a gallows built, seventy-five feet high, and ask the king in the morning to have Mordecai hanged on it. Then go with the king to the dinner and *be happy*." This suggestion *delighted* Haman, and he had the gallows built' (5:14).

Character defects matter. God uses the make-up of even wicked men against them. They ruin themselves in their folly. 'A man's own folly ruins his life, yet his heart rages against the LORD' (Proverbs 19:3). 'The LORD works out everything for his own ends — even the wicked for a day of disaster' (Proverbs 16:4).

Little details

The story contains a string of details that, by themselves, are insignificant, and even together might be called 'coincidences'; but they are all integral parts in the plan and purpose of almighty God who 'causes all things to work together for good' for those who love him (Romans 8:28, NASB). These 'coincidences' include the fact that the king could not sleep one night; that the historical records were read out to him; that Mordecai had not been rewarded for saving the king's life; and that Haman just happened to be in the palace early that morning, at just the right time to answer the king's question. God made use of all these things in arranging the deliverance of his people. The net result is that even Haman's wife knew that his ruin was inevitable. Her words of impending doom ring in his ears. 'Since Mordecai, before whom your downfall has started, is of Jewish origin, you cannot stand against him — you will surely come to ruin!' (6:13). No weapon forged against the people of God will prevail. But the fool rushed on in his folly. The reader senses that Haman's end is near.

Irony

We have seen that irony is one of the favourite literary devices of this skilful author. There are more examples not to be missed. There was a mixture of joy and vexation in Haman: 'Haman went out that day happy and in high spirits. But … he was filled with rage against Mordecai' (5:9). This obviously cuts deep because we see it again a few verses later. After boasting that it is only 'the king and I' invited to the party, he added: 'But all this gives me no satisfaction as long as I see that Jew Mordecai sitting at the king's gate' (5:13). Extremely satisfied yet extremely dissatisfied! Adding to the irony, Mordecai is completely at ease. He has finished fasting; the sackcloth is gone and he is in normal clothes again, back at his daily job as a magistrate at the king's gate, and nothing has changed. He still does not bow to this Amalekite, this enemy of God, and he is not the slightest bit afraid of him: 'he neither rose nor showed fear in his presence'. This is a quality to be emulated by all God's people. We do not fear what men might do. Mordecai's attitude was later expressed in Martin Luther's hymn:

And though this world, with devils filled,
    should threaten to undo us,
We will not fear, for God has willed His
    truth to triumph through us.
The prince of darkness grim, we tremble
    not for him;
His rage we can endure, we know his doom
    is sure,
The Word of God shall fell Him.

It is ironic too, and sweet justice, that Haman has to honour his worst enemy! On the same night when the sleepless king remembered he owed his life to Mordecai, Haman built a gallows to murder the king's saviour. Being first at the palace in the early hours of the morning augured well for the success of Haman's murderous request, especially when the king took the initiative to call him. How ironic that the details for honouring Mordecai came out of Haman's own mouth, since he assumed the honours were meant for him. There is further irony in the silliness of the request. Haman could have asked for anything, but what he wanted was to dress up in the king's robes, and ride on the king's horse wearing the king's crest, to be heralded through the streets by a senior official. Such an infantile desire to receive public kudos and adulation is typical of weak men.

It is ironic too that the king did not yet know of the antagonism between Haman and Mordecai. He intended it to be a privilege for Haman to present the 'citizenship award' to Mordecai. Xerxes didn't know what hurt and humiliation it really was for Haman! Having to blow the trumpet of the man you most hate, and having to do it so publicly, must have added salt to his wounds. And think how ridiculous this whole charade must have looked to the ordinary citizens of Persia. They all knew Mordecai and his Jewish friends were on death row! What a joke to parade him around on horseback! The procession would have passed posters on trees and buildings proclaiming their doom. It would have passed Jews everywhere fasting and mourning in sackcloth, and Mordecai would have seen the gallows built for him. Being seventy-five feet high, it towered over the city wall — he could hardly have missed it! But this bizarre procession may have signalled a glimmer of hope to the Jews. Before God destroys Haman he will make a fool of him, filling his cup with gall and vinegar. It made no difference to Mordecai: he returned to his normal duties untroubled. But Haman was utterly peeved: 'Haman rushed home, with his head covered, in grief' (6:12).

There is further irony in the way Haman's closest advisers all 'jumped ship', deserting him. They distanced themselves; they isolated him, conveniently playing down the fact that it was 'party policy' which got Haman into this mess. It was a board decision! He'd followed their advice gladly. But they (rightly) sensed they were going to be on the losing side here. They did not want to know about him. So we are informed: 'His advisers and his wife Zeresh said to him, "Since Mordecai, before whom your downfall has started, is of Jewish origin, you cannot stand against him — you will surely come to ruin!"' (6:13). In other words, 'It is your funeral Haman!' As we all know, twenty-four hours is a long time in politics!

Notice the irony implied in verse 14: 'While they were still talking with him, the king's eunuchs arrived and hurried Haman away to the banquet Esther had prepared.' It seems he was late for it. He was so dismayed at the mess he was in that messengers had to hurry him away. Normally he would have been there early. This is the banquet he had been crowing about, Esther's banquet for just 'the king and I'. Now it was the last thing he wanted. But he could not afford to refuse dining with the two most important people in Persia. What a bitter pill! He would have been anything but scintillating company at the table!

The literary brilliance of this book of Esther is beginning to dawn upon us.

QUESTIONS FOR DISCUSSION

1. Read Isaiah 54 for words of comfort spoken to Israel in her seventy years of exile in Babylon. What principles of comfort apply to God's people in Esther's time and ours?

2. 'Godly living is a mixture of trusting God's sovereign rule while we act responsibly.' Is that true? Before answering, read Philippians 2:12-13; Ephesians 6:10-18; and 1 Thessalonians 1:3-10.

3. Read Romans 1:18-21 and 2:4-11. How do these texts show that neither Haman nor anyone else has an excuse for opposing God?

CHAPTER SEVEN

'HANG HIM!'

LOOK IT UP

BIBLE READING

Esther 7

INTRODUCTION

The truth had finally come home to the King of Persia that his prime minister was a dreadful man. When it was pointed out that Haman had built gallows seventy-five feet high, to murder the man who had saved the king's life, Xerxes needed no time to deliberate. 'The king said, "Hang him on it!"' (v. 9). So justice was dispensed immediately.

Keep in mind that this was the climax of the two banquets that Haman had been crowing about. It must have rocked him to the core to hear those damning words from the most powerful ruler on earth: 'Hang him! Get rid of this man from the land of the living! String him up on his own grotesque construction! Haman wants a public hanging; let him be the star of the show!' Our God uses human instruments in keeping his oath against the Amalekites. As we study how chapter 7 sets out the process leading to this well-deserved end, we can divide the story into three categories:

1. The charge
2. The judgement
3. The execution

The charge

The scene is the second private banquet that Esther arranged for Xerxes and Haman. She has promised to tell the king what has been bothering her. It was not an easy situation for her. Just how do you tell a king that his handpicked prime minister is rotten to the core? But we have seen how Esther was a woman of faith and courage, and how she had shown wisdom and humility in preparing an opportunity. Now her moment has come.

'As they were drinking wine on that second day, the king again asked, "Queen Esther, what is your petition? It will be given you. What is your request? Even up to half the kingdom, it will be granted."' She cannot keep Xerxes in suspense any longer. The indictment against Haman has to be stated. He has to be charged face to face. So she responded:

> If I have found favour with you, O king, and if it pleases your majesty, grant me my life — this is my petition. And spare my people — this is my request. For I and my people have been sold for destruction and slaughter and annihilation. If we had merely been sold as male and female slaves,

I would have kept quiet, because no such distress would justify disturbing the king (vv. 3-4).

Notice several commendable features here.

Succinct

Esther is brief and to the point. She spelled out the mortal danger facing herself and the Jewish people. What a shock it must have been for Xerxes to hear her pleading, 'Grant me my life!' What a shock for a husband to discover that some wretch wants to murder his wife. It may well have taken his mind back a few years, when his own life was under threat, and he executed the two conspirators. Let's not read over these words without understanding their impact. Put yourself in the situation. When Esther said, 'Grant me my life ... and spare my people,' it was like finding the missing piece in a jigsaw puzzle. Now the king could see the full picture. Now a whole number of facts dawned upon him for the first time. Now Xerxes discovered that Esther was a Jew. And now he realized that he had been bribed and deceived by Haman into authorizing the annihilation of her people. A few minutes later (when Harbona pointed out the gallows intended for Mordecai) he realized that Mordecai was a Jew. Presumably he now realized that Haman's

WHAT THE TEXT TEACHES

offer of 10,000 talents of silver was just a bribe (3:9). That is what Esther was referring to when she said, 'I and my people have been *sold* for destruction.'

Regardless of what you think of Xerxes' character (and we have seen some unflattering realities about him in the story so far), we can easily imagine the distress he now felt in realizing that Haman had manoeuvred him to permit a law that, unwittingly, ensured the death penalty for his own wife.

Shrewdly anonymous

Esther is careful not to name Haman as the villain. She factually describes his genocidal wickedness using the very words in the decree posted throughout the empire: destruction and slaughter and annihilation. This was a clever tactic because it left the king to decide objectively on the merits of the case without any names being involved. It avoids any possibility of personal bias leading the king to excuse the crime. And it paid dividends. When Xerxes immediately asked, 'Who is he? Where is the man who has dared to do such a thing?' it is obvious that the king is on her side. Xerxes has correctly judged the anonymous perpetrator to be an audacious criminal. He demands his name and address and he wants no delay. Xerxes intends to bring whoever did this to justice. Then it was appropriate for Esther to remove the veil of anonymity. She charged Haman openly and fearlessly: 'The adversary and enemy is this vile Haman.' The man he is hunting is sitting next to

him at the table. She explicitly calls Haman 'vile', sensing that Xerxes would have to agree.

Dignified

She shows dignified respect for the king's office. Apologetically, she indicates her reluctance to bother the king, saying it is only the seriousness of the matter that caused her to petition him. This is evident in the second part of verse 4: 'If we had merely been sold as male and female slaves, I would have kept quiet, because no such distress would justify disturbing the king.' This is a tricky piece of Hebrew to translate because the word 'distress' (צָר) can also mean 'enemy' or 'adversary' and the other key word (נֵזֶק) occurs only here in the entire Old Testament. It refers to 'loss' or 'injury' or 'damage' of some sort. So the NIV translation is possible, and the meaning is then that Esther would not create a 'loss' or 'injury' to the king's valuable time by bothering him with a relatively small problem, not even the problem of slavery.

However the marginal note in the NIV reflects another possibility: 'But the compensation our adversary offers cannot be compared with the loss the king would suffer.' In other words, 'No matter what compensation the king might gain if Haman destroys us Jews, nothing can make up for the loss he will suffer.' In this case Esther

WHAT THE TEXT TEACHES

is not talking about wasting the king's time, but ruining the king's reputation. No amount of money will make up for his loss if the Jews are exterminated from the Persian Empire. The reasons implied probably include the following points.

a. Jews are loyal and industrious citizens, not rebels as Haman falsely claimed (3:8). The obvious proof is that they were free to return to Israel but volunteered to remain. Indeed, the king owes his life to Mordecai the Jew.

b. Who will ever trust Xerxes again if he honours Mordecai for saving his life one day but executes him the next? Who will ever care about his life again? If another plot to kill him is discovered, they may well think, 'I don't care if it succeeds, Xerxes has proved himself dishonourable. Why save a man who executes his saviours?'

c. Xerxes will be known as the king who not only appointed a murderer as his prime minister, but who tolerated being deceived by him to pass a major law, and who did nothing about it when he discovered the facts. 'Xerxes is weak' will be the headlines.

d. Xerxes will be known as a man who repeatedly promised his queen 'up to half his kingdom' but who refused to deliver simple justice. And what sort of fool passes a law that destroys his wife?

This latter understanding (in the NIV margin) seems the most likely, but either way, Esther showed great skill in choosing words that would be most likely to minimize offence, maintain dignity and achieve a good result.

REMEMBER THIS

Here is a valuable life-skill to learn.

'Through patience a ruler can be persuaded, and a gentle tongue can break a bone' (Proverbs 25:15). Esther demonstrates the wisdom of patiently seeking the right moment, and 'a gentle tongue' that persuades most and offends least. The Bible not only exhorts us to speak the truth, but to speak it in the most constructive way possible. 'Do not let any unwholesome talk come out of your mouths, but only what is helpful for building others up according to their needs, that it may benefit those who listen' (Ephesians 4:29).

The judgement

The judgement was obvious before it was announced. In fact there is no need for the guilty verdict to be pronounced. There was no enquiry;

the king did not ask Haman if he had anything to say. And there was no protest from Haman. He knew he was finished as soon as Esther named him. 'Then Haman was terrified before the king and queen. The king got up in a rage, left his wine and went out into the palace garden. But Haman, realizing that the king had already decided his fate, stayed behind to beg Queen Esther for his life' (vv. 6-7).

That moment was a steep learning curve for Haman too. Only then did he realize that Esther was a Jew. Only then did it dawn on him what he has done to Xerxes. Now all his lies and malice return to haunt him. 'Haman was terrified,' and what terror it must have been. Imagine the dry mouth, the nervous posture, the sinking feeling, and the utter discomfort. Where could he look? What could he say? His recent embarrassing humiliation (leading Mordecai in honour through the streets) seemed trivial now that he has discovered that he has unwittingly conspired to kill the Queen of Persia. Those prestigious 'king and I' banquets are now his worst nightmare. What a pitiful sight we see next.

When the enraged king went into the garden to gather his thoughts, Haman stayed behind to beg Queen Esther for his life. The one who so callously plotted the death of thousands was now a snivelling coward begging a woman for mercy. He, who resented one Jew not bowing to him, is now crawling before a Jew. He was begging his life from one of the many whose life he would have taken. In doing so, there was no indication of any apology, no confession of criminality,

WHAT THE TEXT TEACHES

and no recognition of the truth of the charges against him and of the penalty demanded by justice. There is nothing that even resembled the traitor Judas Iscariot's 'I have sinned'. All we see here is a fawning, snivelling coward who wants to avoid justice, afraid to die. Haman has no dignity, not even in his death.

The supreme irony is that his impassioned plea for mercy actually signed his death warrant. We read: 'Just as the king returned from the palace garden to the banquet hall, Haman was falling on the couch where Esther was reclining. The king exclaimed: "Will he even molest the queen while she is with me in the house?" As soon as the word left the king's mouth, they covered Haman's face' (v. 8). The point is that protocols for a harem were very strict in the ancient Near East. It was improper for Haman to remain in the room alone with the queen when the king had departed. No one knew that better than Haman, and he surely would have left with the king had he not been so desperate. By approaching her as she reclined on her couch this opportunist went too far. The phrase 'falling on the couch' presumably means that he flung himself at her mercy; he collapsed face down at her feet. But from where the king stood on his way back from the garden it looked like a sexual assault.

Ironically again, even if Esther was willing to help Haman, there was nothing she could do. It was too late now that the king had seen this. Even if she was willing to grant clemency regarding his plot against the Jews, *that* crime is not the issue now. It is the apparent sexual molestation that has enraged the king. There is more irony in that Haman tried to escape death for crimes he *did* commit yet he was executed for a crime he *did not* commit. But will anyone protest that justice was not done? Of course not.

It is clear too that the king has no doubts about Haman's thorough wickedness. We can see that in his indignant question: 'Will he even molest the queen while she is with me in the house?' In other words, 'I know Haman will stoop to the gross crimes already charged against him, but will he not stop there? Does he have no common decency at all?' And then we are told, 'As soon as the word left the king's mouth, they covered Haman's face.' This was a custom in the ancient Near East. The heads of condemned prisoners were covered, indicating they were on death row. It also shows that even at a small private function the king always had his 'minders' close by.

The execution

By covering Haman's face, the king's servants not only anticipated the capital punishment about to come, but one of them even anticipated the method. Harbona told the king about the new high-rise structure in town: 'Then Harbona ... said, "A gallows seventy-five feet high stands by Haman's house. He had it made for Mordecai,

WHAT THE TEXT TEACHES

who spoke up to help the king.'" So Xerxes took the hint as good advice. 'The king said, "Hang him on it!" So they hanged Haman on the gallows he had prepared for Mordecai. Then the king's fury subsided.' What poetic justice! What a good illustration of the truth in Proverbs 26:27: 'If a man digs a pit, he will fall into it.'

There is a practical application for us here. Those who rise up to oppose the death penalty need to think again. What answer will they give to this situation in Esther? Absolutely everything in this book points to the propriety of Haman's execution. How appropriate, how fitting, how deserved, how utterly just and right. It is in full accord with the Lord's moral command for society when it recommenced after the Flood: 'And surely I will require your lifeblood; from every beast I will require it. And from every man, from every man's brother I will require the life of man. "Whoever sheds man's blood, by man his blood shall be shed, For in the image of God he made man"' (Genesis 9:5-6, NASB).

'Hang him!' And with those words justice was done. But it is more than justice here. Remember, this is a covenant issue. It is a vindication of Mordecai's refusal to bow to Haman: 'When the LORD your God gives you rest from all the enemies around you in the land he is giving you to possess as an inheritance, you shall blot out the memory of Amalek from under heaven. Do not forget!' (Deuteronomy 25:19). Mordecai did not forget, and though he had no authority to execute the Amalekite, Xerxes did, and God arranged the circumstances so that it was carried out. All praise to God for his faithfulness, his justice and his governing over all history.

QUESTIONS FOR DISCUSSION

1. Read Psalm 73. How does it help us to cope with wicked men like Haman?

2. How does Haman's execution display God's justice? See Proverbs 11:8 and 26:27.

3. How secure are secrets? See Ecclesiastes 12:14; Romans 2:16, Hebrews 4:13; Luke 12:2-3; and 1 Corinthians 4:5.

4. How significant is confession of sins? See Psalm 32:1-5; Psalm 51:1-4; and 1 John 1:8-9.

CHAPTER EIGHT

THE OIL OF JOY
FOR MOURNING

LOOK IT UP

BIBLE READING

Esther 8

INTRODUCTION

While Isaiah was not specifically thinking of the events in Esther 8, his words provide an excellent assessment of that historic scene:

The LORD has anointed me to preach good news to the poor. He has sent me to bind up the broken-hearted, to proclaim freedom for the captives and release from darkness for the prisoners, to proclaim the year of the LORD's favour and the day of vengeance of our God, to comfort all who mourn and provide for those who grieve Zion — to bestow on them a crown of beauty instead of ashes, the oil of gladness instead of mourning, and a garment of praise instead of a spirit of despair. They will be called oaks of righteousness, a planting of the LORD for the display of his splendour (Isaiah 61:1-3).

Isaiah is talking about exactly the same thing as the book of Esther, namely, how almighty God delivers his covenant people from death. So it is the gospel theme. Behind the scenes of Persian history, God was at work delivering his people from the malice of Haman the Amalekite. What contrasts we see in chapter 8 compared to the miseries earlier in the story! The Jews had been fasting and mourning in sackcloth and ashes but now they rejoice. God has given them 'beauty instead of ashes, the oil of gladness instead of mourning, and a garment of praise instead of a spirit of despair'. Extensive changes have taken place, especially:

1. Changes in government
2. Changes in law
3. Changes in attitudes

Changes in government

Property rights

The removal of Haman 'the horrible' brought about a number of administrative changes. It was common in the ancient Near East for all the property of condemned criminals to revert to the Crown. No heirs would get a windfall from the estate of a criminal relative. So we are told, 'That same day King Xerxes gave Queen Esther the estate of Haman, the enemy of the Jews.' How that would have irked Haman if he had still been alive — a Jew having control of his entire property! The writer makes it very clear where his sympathy lies, underscoring the inherent justice of it by stressing that Haman was the enemy of the Jews. So it illustrates the Proverb, 'a sinner's wealth is stored up for the righteous' (Proverbs 13:22).

In case anyone is inclined to feel sorry for his widow Zeresh, do not trouble yourself unduly. She was the one who came up with the murderous idea of building a gallows for lynching Mordecai, even specifying that it be seventy-five feet high! Her disinheritance is well deserved! By placing Haman's estate in Esther's hands we know that Xerxes has a high regard for her. She is not just a pretty face. Her courage and wisdom have impressed him.

A promotion

The next change was a promotion for Mordecai. A magistrate already, he was now made prime minister in Haman's place. 'Mordecai came into the presence of the king, for Esther had told how he was related to her. The king took off his signet ring, which he had reclaimed from Haman, and presented it to Mordecai.' This allowed Mordecai to act with regal authority, sealing orders so that they not only became law, but irrevocable and binding law. Mordecai's promotion to the heights is a complete contrast to Haman's fall. And, as a double honour, Esther lost no time in making him sole executor of Haman's estate.

Legal prerogatives

These changes were not merely bureaucratic paper shuffling. The proof is seen in the legal prerogatives entrusted to Mordecai and Esther. After hearing Esther's impassioned plea for the Jews, Xerxes agreed that a new law was needed to get around the tragic massacre involved in Haman's earlier law against the Jews. This new law will be an important law and will need careful framing, yet Xerxes was happy to entrust all the details to Mordecai and Esther. He took no part in it himself. He told them: 'Now write another decree in the king's name on behalf of the Jews as seems best to you, and seal it with the king's signet ring — for no document written in the king's name and sealed with his ring can be revoked' (v. 8). Xerxes was happy to have his name on any law written by Esther and Mordecai. This is profound trust indeed, especially since he had had his fingers burnt trusting Haman. But there was no 'once bitten, twice shy' here. These were people of proven calibre.

High ratings

Commensurate with his high position, Mordecai dressed in regal garments (what a contrast to the sackcloth and ashes of recent days): 'Mordecai left the king's presence wearing royal garments of blue and white, a large crown of gold and a purple robe of fine linen. And the city of Susa held a joyous celebration' (v. 15).

That last comment is interesting because it shows Mordecai had a high approval rating, and not only among Jews. The general population of the Persian capital was very happy that Mordecai had replaced Haman. He was obviously a leader who was admired for his decent qualities.

This is an outstanding achievement given that Mordecai was especially known for his loyalty to his own Jewish people. In fact the book closes on that note: 'Mordecai the Jew was second in rank to King Xerxes, preeminent among the Jews, and held in high esteem by his many fellow Jews, because he worked for the good of his people and spoke up for the welfare of all the Jews' (10:3). So his love for Israel was not at the expense of concern for Persians or any other racial group. His racial affiliation was not racial prejudice. This man was a fair and honourable neighbour to everyone. Here we see an illustration of Proverbs 29:2: 'When the righteous thrive, the people rejoice; when the wicked rule, the people groan.' As a practical parallel, Christians should be active in supporting true Christianity but not at the expense of genuine love for other neighbours.

Changes in law

We now get another insight into Esther's admirable qualities. Although she has already pleaded for the welfare of her Jewish people, Xerxes had been so preoccupied with removing the threat to her life that nothing had been done to help the other Jews. An inferior character might have left well alone now that she was personally safe. No one will dare to harm her now that Haman has been executed. But she is a person of substance, so she pours out her intercession for Israel in a deeply moving request.

> Esther again pleaded with the king, falling at his feet and weeping. She begged him to put an end to the evil plan of Haman the Agagite, which he had devised against the Jews. Then the king extended the gold sceptre to Esther and she arose and stood before him. 'If it pleases the king,' she said, 'and if he regards me with favour and thinks it the right thing to do, and if he is pleased with me, let an order be written overruling the dispatches that Haman son of Hammedatha, the Agagite, devised and wrote to destroy the Jews in all the king's provinces. For how can I bear to see disaster fall on my people? How can I bear to see the destruction of my family?' (vv. 3-6).

The king agreed with her plea and immediately ordered the writing of a new law. A number of features stand out.

Emphatic trust

The exact words of Xerxes are more emphatic than 'write another decree in the king's name' as our translations have it in verse 8. The Hebrew actually has 'And *you*, *you* write another decree' (וְאַתֶּם כִּתְבוּ), not only repeating the pronoun but making it the first word, for particular emphasis. In other words, not only does the king want Mordecai and Esther to write the new legislation, but he does not want anyone else involved, not even himself. How many heads of State are willing to extend that degree of confidence and trust to their representatives? We all understand that, in our system of parliamentary government, ministers of departments are ultimately responsible for the actions of the public servants in their portfolio. But throughout history many ministers have been embarrassed by that system of trust. Portfolios have been lost as the consequence of incompetent bureaucrats. But Xerxes does not fear coming unstuck from any incompetence in Mordecai or Esther. Their wisdom is evident in the details of the legislation. Notice some of the features.

Suitable limitations

There was no killing spree allowed here. Jews were not permitted an equal and opposite massacre to the one Haman's brought against them. No, they were simply given the right of self-defence: 'The king's edict granted the Jews in every city the right to assemble and protect themselves' (v. 11). Even the definition of self-defence was stipulated, namely: 'to destroy, kill and annihilate any armed force of any nationality or province that might attack them and their women and children; and to plunder the property of their enemies'. There were to be no civilian targets! They were not to act like the infamous Lieutenant William Calley, who machine-gunned a Vietnamese village full of old men, women and children in the infamous My Lai Massacre on 16 March 1968. The Jews were granted the right to de-stroy only aggressive military targets: 'any armed force of any nationality or province that might attack them and their women and children'. This law was no threat to Persians generally, no threat to ordinary civilians or innocent bystanders. The message was: 'Leave the Jews alone and they'll leave you alone.'

This is part of a much larger ethic of self-defence. Pacifism is not a biblical option. It is the duty of an individual to take all proper steps to preserve life and property — his own and that of others.[1]

Secondly, the law applied for twenty-four hours only. They were granted just one day for defending them-selves so it could be laid to rest and not escalate into an ongoing vendetta. So, 'The day appointed for the Jews to do this in all the provinces of King Xerxes was the thirteenth day of the twelfth month, the month of Adar' (v. 12). For reasons we'll consider soon, there was an extension of one more day granted, but only in the city of Susa: 'Esther said, "If it pleases the king, let to-morrow also be granted to the Jews who are in Susa to

WHAT THE TEXT TEACHES

do according to the edict of today; and let Haman's ten sons be hanged on the gallows." So the king commanded that it should be done so; and an edict was issued in Susa, and Haman's ten sons were hanged' (9:13-14).

The Jews showed considerable restraint in carrying out this law. In particular they refused to take advantage of their permission to 'plunder the property of their enemies'. They did not pillage or loot or enrich themselves (though Haman certainly intended to plunder them and had specified it in his terrible law). The writer takes pains to show us this Jewish restraint by mentioning it three times: 'but they did not lay their hands on the plunder' (9:10,15,16). In an empire where laws were permanent, unable to be repealed, this new law shows the commendable wisdom of Esther and Mordecai. They were certainly the right people raised up by God for the needs of the hour.

THINK ABOUT IT

There's an important ethic here. God is committed to justice. 'Let the punishment fit the crime' is a popular way of stating the Bible's ethic of 'eye for eye and tooth for tooth'. This is the law of retribution (*lex talionis*). The gospel does not dispel criminal

justice. Jesus did not revoke that principle of justice in Matthew 5:38-42. Rather he spoke out
against private individuals taking the law into their
own hands, taking revenge. That is not our private
task. We are to love our neighbour, desiring the
very best for him, even when we co-operate with
the police as they arrest him for crimes. But the
civil government must carry out justice. It is God's
avenger. Its penalties must be neither excessive
nor inadequate, but appropriate for the crime. The
ethic 'eye for eye' is a universal moral ethic for all
civil rulers.

Changes in attitudes

A whole new set of moods and attitudes swept over
Persia. We have already noted how 'the city of Susa
held a joyous celebration'. The Jews no longer mourned
and fasted on death row. The new law has changed all
that: 'For the Jews it was a time of happiness and joy,
gladness and honour. In every province and in every
city, wherever the edict of the king went, there was joy
and gladness among the Jews, with feasting and celebrating' (vv. 16-17). But then we read something surprising: 'And many people of other nationalities became
Jews because fear of the Jews had seized them.' How
are we to understand that?

There are two pitfalls to avoid here. On the one hand,
there is a cynical view saying that this was dissimulation,

not genuine, only a matter of convenience. It claims there were no genuine conversions to Judaism or to Yahweh, the God of Israel. Rather, it was just a pragmatic policy of 'If you can't beat them, join them.'

On the other hand it would be unrealistic (even gullible) to assume that every one of these 'conversions' was based on religious convictions. Undoubtedly there were many who aligned themselves with Israel for purely pragmatic reasons of self-interest. The verb used here to describe this action is literally 'they Judaised themselves' (מִתְיַהֲדִים). So there was some degree of pragmatic convenience but we should not deny there were some genuine conversions.

To keep some perspective, it is good to recall that this was not the only time foreigners had joined themselves to Israel. Ruth the Moabite did so out of conviction. So did Rahab in Jericho, and the New Testament lists her as a 'hero of faith'. So also did Uriah the Hittite. And we should not forget the significant number of Egyptians who joined with Israel at the Exodus. The ten plagues in Egypt were irrefutable evidence to Pharaoh's advisers that 'the finger of God' was upon them (Exodus 8:19). Presumably, here in Persia too, people were stunned by the recent events and the dramatic changes that followed. Many of them may also have sensed 'the finger of God'. Some of them would have realized that the God of Israel was fighting for his people as he had done so many times before.

We see evidence for this in Zeresh, Haman's wife. When he came home complaining about his humiliation at Mordecai's citizenship award, she, with his other advisers, told him: 'Since Mordecai, before whom your downfall has started, is of Jewish origin, you cannot stand against him — you will surely come to ruin!' (6:13). What drove her to that conclusion? It was her knowledge of the history of Israel. The Persians knew how God had delivered his people from one hopeless situation after another. They all knew about Egypt and Jericho and the conquest of Palestine. Nation after nation had learned the hard way about harming Israel: Ammonites, Hittites, Jebusites and Philistines all bore scars. Closer to home, Zeresh knew about the Babylonian captivity and how Jehovah had humbled Nebuchadnezzar like an animal, and how he had protected Daniel in the lion's den, and Shadrack, Meshack and Abednego in the fiery furnace. You cannot keep such things secret.

It is safe to say that Zeresh was no ardent convert when she warned Haman. She was not preaching a sermon. She was no devout Jew. But even she knew enough Jewish history so that, in the light of current events in Persia, she could put two and two together. She could see the hand of God again. So she told her husband he was a fool: 'You have already begun to fall before Mordecai and you will continue to fall before him simply because he is a Jew. Don't you know that

WHAT THE TEXT TEACHES

the God of Israel fights for his people? Your humiliation has only just begun, Haman. Quit while you are ahead.' As Isaiah said, 'No weapon forged against you will prevail' (Isaiah 54:17).

The text says that many people sided with the Jews because 'fear of the Jews had seized them'. Perhaps that meant the Jews had a reputation for being very good fighters, especially when the 'chips' are down. Or perhaps they feared the prospect of Yahweh defending the Jews. Either way, their fear was sensible in the light of recent events. Those who still chose to attack the Jews in loyalty to Haman were asking for a hiding! And as it happens, they got it.

Some people may be cynical because of the current situation in the Middle East. In Iran today (Persia became Iran in 1935) there is an official doctrine of dissimulation, meaning that a person is entitled to deny his religion and pose as a member of some other faith if confronted with acute personal danger. The Shiite Moslems of Iran are permitted to pose as Sunnites when they take their pilgrimage to Mecca, because Mecca is controlled by the Sunnites who have sometimes been violent to Shiites. In Iran generally, religious minorities frequently pose as Shiites for protection. It is a socially-accepted custom. But again, there is no reason to read Esther 8:17 in that way.

Something should be said about why Esther (on Mordecai's instructions, 2:10) had concealed her Jewish identity. She has been charged with dissimulation, a lack of faith, and dishonouring God. Her critics say she should have been more like Daniel who deliberately publicized his Jewish convictions by praying to Yahweh in front of an open window. However, the comparison is invalid. Daniel was in captivity and was expected to worship Babylonian gods. Esther's generation was not in captivity, was free to return home, and was free to worship God. Persian Jews would have been foolish to flaunt their ethnic-minority distinctives. To refuse a reasonable degree of assimilation would be divisive. When in Rome, do what the Romans do!

In any case it is obvious that there was a widespread undercurrent of anti-Semitism in Persia. Haman's attitude was not isolated. It was the tip of the iceberg, as evidenced by his ability to count on Persians everywhere to join in the slaughter of Jews. Plainly, the Jews were recognizable. They could never hide their culture in a foreign land. It wasn't only certain physical attributes that identified them plainly as Jews. Their language, their accent, their values and the kosher diet all contributed. So Esther and others are falsely accused of dissimulation. They were not involved in a shameful concealing of their Jewishness. Rather, they wisely refrained from provocatively flaunting it in a foreign land. Christians would do well to recognize the same principle. When questioned, we should not hesitate to declare our allegiance to Christ, and our life should show it. But it is not wise to be parading our Christianity in an aggressive, provocative manner that needlessly stirs up the natives of the land.

Let us never forget how God rules and over-rules in human history, working all things for the good of his covenant people. Ultimately he will dry away every tear and remove every hurt and 'everlasting joy shall be upon their head'. Until then, let the message of Esther strengthen our resolve to trust him completely.

QUESTIONS FOR DISCUSSION

DISCUSS IT

1. How important are good rulers? See 2 Samuel 23:3-4; Proverbs 29:2.

2. How do the following texts help us assess the genuineness of Persian converts? See Psalm 67; Zechariah 8:20-23; Revelation 5:9; 13:7.

3. How do the following texts show that Christianity upholds strict legal justice? See Matthew 7:2; Romans 2:11-12; 2 Corinthians 5:10; Colossians 3:25; Revelation 2:23.

THE GUIDE

CHAPTER NINE

'NO ONE COULD STAND AGAINST THEM'

LOOK IT UP

BIBLE READING

Esther 9:1-17

INTRODUCTION

What a strange situation it was when the day of battle finally arrived, 'the thirteenth day of the twelfth month, the month of Adar': strange because neither side could be called 'rebels', neither side was illegal. On one side were the followers of Haman, the deceased ex-prime minister of Persia; standing against them were all the Jews in Persia; and each group had the law of Persia on its side. Each group had authority to kill the other group, an authority that was written down in black and white with the king's seal on it. It certainly shows the danger of a legal system without proper checks and balances. It highlights the folly of the Medo-Persian system where laws could not be repealed, corrected or amended. Let us never underestimate the blessings of living in a system where laws can be changed.

The outcome was a decisive victory for the Jews, celebrated every year since by the Feast of Purim created for that very purpose (9:20-32).

The Jewish victory was unexpected: 'the enemies of the Jews had hoped to overpower them' (v. 1) but they were humiliated. The result is described in various ways: 'The tables were turned and the Jews got the upper hand over those who hated them… No one could stand against them… The Jews struck down all their enemies with the sword, killing and destroying them, and they did what they pleased to those who hated them' (vv. 1,2,5).

This whole episode has attracted a great deal of mis-guided criticism. That, again, is the inevitable conse-quence of taking a moralistic, rather than covenantal, approach to the Old Testament. We can get a deeper understanding of this part of Scripture by considering some of the criticisms made against this historic day of Jewish victory when 'no one could stand against them'.

The three major criticisms of this text concern:

1. The 75,000 Persian casualties (v. 16)
2. The hanging of ten corpses, Haman's sons (vv. 13-14)
3. The extra day granted to allow the Jews to kill another 300 enemies (vv. 13-14).

The 75,000 Persian casualties

In addition to the 500 men killed in the city of Susa, we are told: 'Meanwhile, the remainder of the Jews who were in the king's provinces also assembled to protect

themselves and get relief from their enemies. They killed seventy-five thousand of them but did not lay their hands on the plunder' (v. 16). It is of course likely to be a rounded number. The literal statistic may have been 73,864 (for instance), which is rounded up to 75,000. That is a common feature of all literature, and is not a problem.

An impossible figure?

But, even allowing for that, the criticism commonly alleged here is that the Bible is wrong because the Jews could not possibly have killed as many as 75,000 in a single day, and the Persian Government would not have tolerated such slaughter against its own citizens. In answering this, we should notice that it is very precarious reasoning to insist that the *unusual* is equivalent to the *impossible!* Yes, this event is quite unusual, but everything in the context makes it possible, very possible.

For a start, the casualties would have been even greater if Haman's original law had gone unchallenged. Every single Jew in Persia would be dead. Given that only a small minority of Jews returned to Palestine at the start of the Persian Empire, we are looking at considerably more than 75,000. How many? We can make a reasonable estimate from the figures given in

Ezra 2:64 and Nehemiah 7:66, where we learn that there were 42,360 Jews who returned to Israel from Babylonian exile. We know that these expatriates were a very small minority, probably less than 10%. When you allow for the 114 years that have passed under Persian rule, there were at least 500,000 Jews in Persia! So Persian law had decreed the mass slaughter of half a million people in a single day! How would the critics cope with that? We must keep our eye on the true proportions here!

To say that the Persian Government would never tolerate such slaughter of its own citizens is astonishing. The Jews *were* its own citizens! The Prime Minister (with the king's authorization) not only tolerated but decreed the wholesale slaughter of that entire ethnic group! This is radical ethnic cleansing! That makes Saddam Hussein look humane! Persia was made up of citizens from numerous languages, cultures and nationalities, the former citizens of the Babylonian Empire. Moreover, ancient history testifies abundantly to very callous attitudes to human life by Persian leaders, especially where members of the royal family were involved. So the criticism has no credibility.

In any case, a simple calculation will show how realistic the figure of 75,000 is. We are told several times that Persia was a vast empire of 127 provinces stretching all the way from India to Ethiopia. We know that 800 fell in just one city alone, Susa. What about the other 126 provinces (each made up of many cities, towns, villages, and rural communities)? It only requires an average of 600 in each province to give a total of 75,000. So the figure is quite realistic.

A sick joke?

Another approach comes from Bruce Jones who regards the 75,000 as a deliberate exaggeration put in by the writer for humorous effect. He says, 'If an enemy did not attack the Jews first, he was in no danger. Who would be so foolish as to make himself subject to the second edict? It would be suicide to attack the Jews … the answer is that 800 people in Susa and 75,000 in the provinces were so stupid! It is unfortunate that so many readers have failed to see that the account is a deliberate hyperbole.'[1] In other words, Jones claims it is a sick joke, exaggeration being used as a cynical way of making a point. The author says in effect: 'Have a guess how many fools there were in Persia? Answer, 800 in Susa and 75,000 in the rest of the country! Sure, and pigs might fly.'

The trouble is that the writer of this book is noted for the exact opposite style. We do not find him overstating things. At the most he relies on a very matter-of-fact narration, but frequently he leaves readers to draw out the implications for themselves. God's name is not mentioned in this book, but it is obvious that he is behind the scenes delivering his covenant people. We have seen repeatedly the use of irony (the art of understating the conclusions) as one of the

favourite techniques. Of all the writers in the entire
Bible, the last one you would attribute exaggeration to
is the writer of Esther. So the criticism lacks credibility.

However, Jones faces two other major difficulties.
Firstly, he is forced to concede that if there is exaggeration here then there was exaggeration in Haman's
decree too. In other words, the edict 'to destroy, kill,
and annihilate all the Jews — young and old, women
and little children — on a single day, the thirteenth
day of the twelfth month, the month of Adar, and to
plunder their goods' (3:13) is not to be taken seriously
either. It is simply an exaggerated way of saying 'Haman
intended to cause trouble for the Jews.' Jones is way
out of line here. It is obvious that the author intends it
to be taken literally. Everything in the context and genre
suggests literal precision, and nothing suggests anything different. It is the literal horror of Haman's decree that alone explains what follows: the grief and
trauma of the Jews, the fasting in sackcloth and ashes,
the courageous faith of Mordecai and Esther, and the
yearly Purim celebrations.

Secondly, if the figure of 75,000 is only a joke, what
is the writer actually trying to say? According to Jones
the real message is: 'Because the population of Persia
could see the tables had turned, and fear of Mordecai
and the Jews had gripped them, and because they were
not idiots, the day itself turned out to be an anticlimax. There were very few casualties because very few
people attacked the Jews, and the few who did got what
they deserved for being so mad.' How then does the
feast of Purim make sense? The climax of the book is

the sheer ecstasy and joy and celebration of the Jews in their victory. They were not celebrating a day of anticlimax, a day when most of Persia was docile, just a few back-yard brawls with a small minority of slow learners. They were celebrating a massive victory against terrible odds.

The language explaining the annual feast of Purim begs that interpretation. The whole point of it was 'to ... celebrate annually the fourteenth and fifteenth days of the month of Adar as the time when the Jews got relief from their enemies, and as the month when their sorrow was turned into joy and their mourning into a day of celebration ... to observe the days as days of feasting and joy and giving presents of food to one another and gifts to the poor. So the Jews agreed to continue the celebration they had begun... For Haman ... the Agagite, the enemy of all the Jews, had plotted against the Jews to destroy them and had cast the *pur* (that is, the lot) for their ruin and destruction' (vv. 21-24). So the criticism makes no sense. No sane person exaggerates an anticlimax and then describes the annual joyous celebration of it by an entire nation.

Wasn't it 15,000?

Some people are critical of the 75,000 because of the Greek Translation of the Old Testament (known as the *LXX*, or *Septuagint*, after the seventy scholars who produced it about 270 B.C). There, the number is scaled right down to 15,000. Why? We simply do not know. Maybe these Jewish scholars did deliberately understate the total for some reason. Even so, it is a correct statement! There is no contradiction. If the Jews killed 75,000 then they certainly killed 15,000. It does not claim 15,000 as the total number. In any case, the LXX is a translation, and like all translations it is not inspired and not perfect. All translations are fallible works of fallible men. They were translating from the Masoretic (Hebrew) Text, which unambiguously has 75,000 as the figure. So it is no argument to say the LXX has 15,000. That is the same fallacy as criticizing the NIV or NASV because it does not agree with the Authorized Version. No translation is authoritative, only the original manuscripts collectively.

REMEMBER THIS

Our belief in Scripture is non-negotiable.

True Christianity holds to the infallible authority of the sixty-six books of Holy Scripture. Any part is to be understood in harmony with the whole. There are no errors or contradictions. While some parts require special care and expertise, the main truths are so frequently and clearly written that every man can understand what God expects of him and the way of salvation in Christ. Translations vary in accuracy and need to be judged by the Greek and Hebrew manuscripts. To claim that there are mistakes in the Bible is to reject true Christianity.

The hanging of ten corpses

Haman's ten sons were already dead when Esther obtained permission from the king to hang them on the gallows in the capital city. It is interesting that all ten names feature the characteristic 'a' vowel prominent in the names of their father Haman and his forbear, Amalek. Also interesting is the ancient story that says they were hanged one on top of the other! How true that is we do not know, but it does explain something quite unexpected in the Hebrew Bible.

When you come to these ten names (9:7-9) they are listed in a single column, one under the other, on the right-hand side of the page. As a result, there is a large blank space on the left-hand side of this one page in the Hebrew Bible with the list of names 'hanging' down the right-hand side. So the Masoretic scribes who wrote the text obviously liked the ancient story. Thus, every time the book of Esther is opened, the judgement against Haman's posterity hits the reader in the eye, as if to remind us: 'I, the LORD

your God, am a jealous God, punishing the children
for the sin of the fathers to the third and fourth generation of those who hate me, but showing love to a thousand generations of those who love me and keep my
commandments' (Exodus 20:5).

All that aside, what should we say to the torrent of
criticism that this incident has received? Yes, the public hanging of dead bodies is quite extreme but we must
keep this in perspective. Not only was it authorized by
the king, it was requested by no one less than Esther,
whose character in this entire book is impeccable. She
is a model of humility, faith, courage and wisdom. She
is not a vindictive person. Instead of reading it nega-
tively, we should see positive features. At the very least
it was a public warning from the palace that no one is
to harm the Jews again. These hanging bodies mean
the King and Queen of Persia are adamant that anti-
Semitism will not be tolerated while they occupy the
throne.

For those who feel uneasy about this, what are ten
bodies hanging compared to the entire Jewish race lay-
ing dead on the ground? What are ten vile aggressors
compared to the bloodshed they intended for 500,000
men, women and children whose only crime was that
they were Jews? Would any sane man regard it as un-
fair if it was Adolph Hitler hanging there outside his
gas ovens in Auschwitz? No, so we should see this in
exactly the same light!

Let us get away from moralistic interpretation. Let
us continue to see the proper context here. The

giveaway clue is that no one else was hanged, only Haman's line, only the descendants of Amalek. So again we are back to the covenant oath that God had sworn against these inveterate enemies of the church: 'I will completely blot out the memory of Amalek from under heaven... The LORD will be at war against the Amalekites from generation to generation' (Exodus 17:14-16). Esther is acting in accordance with this covenant, aligning herself entirely with God against Amalek.

In any case this is trivial compared to what God will finally do with the enemies of his covenant. They would prefer hanging anytime! Can we not see the emblems of the final judgement here? Just as death did not end it all for Haman's sons, death will not end it for the godless anywhere. There is a judgement after death. There is in fact a second death implied typically by the hanging of the dead. Eternity in hell makes hanging look desirable! The great danger of letting human emotions affect our interpretation of Scripture is that sooner or later it compromises the whole gospel. God's own perfect Son was hung up, not when dead, but while alive until he died! And not by something so kind as a rope, but by cruel metal spikes; and not as a deserving enemy, but innocent, standing in for the enemies and paying their penalty. If we feel at all uneasy at this then we should look at Calvary not Susa! Once human emotion gets into the door of

biblical interpretation, it is a slippery path leading to
the denial of final and ultimate justice: hell itself. If hell
is denied then the cross of Christ is emptied of its glory,
for there he bore the curse of hell for all his people.

The extra day granted to the Jews

Critics miss the point when they complain about the
extra day of self-defence granted by Xerxes to the Jews.
It is clear from the context that Xerxes has no sympathy for the decree he had been tricked into authorizing. He was not amused that he had inadvertently
signed the death warrant for his wife and all her people.
A major injustice had been done and major justice must
redress it. It is also clear that the Hamanite centre of
Jewish hatred is in the capital city itself, close to the
palace. That is where Haman began inciting the bloodshed and that is where his ten sons carried on with it.
So that is where an extra day is needed to make sure
that the malice is thoroughly removed.

Even though the first day saw 500 aggressors struck
down, it is clear that 300 remained. They escaped
justice on day one, but it caught up with them on day
two. Had Xerxes not granted the extra day he would
have been nurturing trouble. Those 300 enemies would
still have been a threat to Esther. As it is, a mere two
days to quell the racial hatred was a very moderate
allocation. The results speak for themselves, making
any criticism odious and embarrassing.

No one could stand against them because almighty God was fighting for them. He had been working behind the scenes of history to bring about this glorious victory for his people. No one can withstand God. God assures his people 'No weapon forged against you will prosper' (Isaiah 54:17). In the next chapter we move on to consider some of the other commendable features of that victory.

QUESTIONS FOR DISCUSSION

DISCUSS IT

1. What does the New Testament urge us to learn from the numerous deaths that occurred in Old Testament judgements? See Matthew 24:27-29; 1 Corinthians 10:1-12; Hebrews 3:7-12; 10:28-31.

2. 'To abandon the doctrine of hell is to abandon the gospel.' Evaluate that in the light of the following: Luke 12:4-5; John 3:36; Romans 2:5-10; Ephesians 5:6; Colossians 3:6; Revelation 6:16-17; 14:9-11.

THE GUIDE

CHAPTER TEN

MANY HAPPY RETURNS

BIBLE READING

Esther 9:18 - 10:3

INTRODUCTION

When we say 'Many happy returns' on someone's birthday it means we would like them to return to this day of the year many more times in the future. It is a time for celebration, for looking back over the past with thankfulness, for counting blessings. The book of Esther concludes on a similar note. It is a time of celebration. The Jews in Persia were marvellously delivered from their enemies against all human expectations. It was a sort of birthday, the birth of renewed hope and solidarity. They resolved never to forget it by starting a yearly celebration, the Feast of Purim. There have been many happy returns to this milestone in Jewish history ever since. In fact, Purim has been observed 2,484 times.[1]

At the end of this unique Old Testament book we should notice certain positive and worthwhile points in the victory it celebrates. We have seen why various criticisms levelled against the Jews in their victory have no credibility and should not detract from the celebrations that close the book on a high note. Three matters are worth noting:

1. The fine performance
2. The feast of Purim
3. The finishing touches

The fine performance

In celebrating their victory over Haman, the Jews could hold their heads up. They had nothing to be ashamed of. There are two main areas of credit for them in this difficult episode.

1. They were not the aggressors

Those who were intent on carrying out Haman's decree of racial extermination must have been aggressive to the point of fanaticism. Plenty of things should have deterred them, and did deter many other Persians, but they made no difference to these zealots. They remained utterly bloodthirsty. For instance, Haman's death did not hinder them. He was, after all, the instigator and promoter of the bloodbath. It is hard to keep the momentum going for any cause, especially an unjust cause, when the main driving force is gone. So these were very aggressive people.

The recent news that their queen was a Jew did nothing to deter them from killing Jews. Neither that nor her support from King Xerxes sobered them at all. This makes their aggression a form of treachery, fighting against the ruling palace. Those in important official positions were certainly sensitive to this: 'All the nobles of the provinces, the satraps, the governors and the king's administrators helped the Jews' (9:3). In other words, a majority of the bureaucracy (including the army) was protecting the Jews. So those who attacked them were seriously bitter and twisted people. Not even the new law or the fact that the population generally sided with the Jews deterred them. Those who attacked the Jews were more than aggressors; they were fanatical, frighteningly irrational, conducting their own insane 'Jihad' like the fundamentalist Islamic terrorists of our times. They were intent on 'ethnic cleansing'. If no one had attacked Israel no one would have been injured, and no one would have died. Let us place the credit where it is due.

2. They showed great restraint

We have already noticed Mordecai and Esther's restraint in stipulating just one day for defending themselves. There would be no ongoing vendetta, and there would be no civilian targets. Only armed aggressors were fought off. But the author also makes the point three times that the Jews did not take advantage of their legal rights to material enrichment: 'but they did not lay their hands on the plunder' (9:10,15,16).

That is to their credit, especially remembering that Mordecai's new law (with royal assent) specifically allowed the Jews 'to plunder the property of their enemies' (8:11). Can you imagine any other fighting force showing such self-restraint? And to the Persians who saw it, such self-denial would be the talk of the town and would do much to commend the Jewish religion to them. It would make it very clear that this was a battle over important principles, rather than materialistic enrichment.

The feast of Purim

Mordecai recorded these events, and he sent letters to all the Jews throughout the provinces of King Xerxes, near and far, to have them celebrate annually the fourteenth and fifteenth days of the month of Adar as the time when the Jews got relief from their enemies, and as the month when their sorrow was turned into joy and their mourning into a day of celebration. He wrote to them to observe the days as days of feasting and joy and giving presents of food to one another and gifts to the poor. So the Jews agreed to continue the celebration they had begun, doing what Mordecai had written to them. For Haman son of Hammedatha, the Agagite, the enemy of all the

WHAT THE TEXT TEACHES

Jews, had plotted against the Jews to destroy them and had cast the *pur* (that is, the lot) for their ruin and destruction... (Therefore these days were called Purim, from the word *pur*.) Because of everything written in this letter and because of what they had seen and what had happened to them, the Jews took it upon themselves to establish the custom that they and their descendants and all who join them should without fail observe these two days every year, in the way prescribed and at the time appointed. These days should be remembered and observed in every generation by every family, and in every province and in every city. And these days of Purim should never cease to be celebrated by the Jews, nor should the memory of them die out among their descendants (vv. 20-28).

The author found it necessary to translate the word *pur* because it is not a Hebrew word but Persian. It reminds us of the radical difference between true and false religion. Haman had cast the *pur* because his religion was superstitious nonsense. He believed (along with pagans generally) that the world is random, that the only 'ruler' is impersonal: 'chance, luck, fortune'. So he would never plan anything major without consulting his 'lucky numbers' (the *pur* referred to wooden cubes like modern dice). But true religion acknowledges that Jehovah-God controls history. The victory of the Jews in Persia settles that. So the feast of Purim signals the stupidity of all superstition, all random-chance views of the universe, all atheistic cosmologies, and the widespread human interest in 'lucky numbers', 'unlucky numbers' and other fetishes.

Research has provided another reason for Christian believers to rejoice. At one time there were critical scholars who ridiculed the book of Esther, claiming that it was not historic fact, being written much later than the Persian period. Why? They claim the feast of Purim was not of Jewish origin but was simply a pagan holiday of fun and feasting which the Jews later adopted. So in order to give it some religious credibility, this book was written. So they say it is fictional, folklore, a story invented to undergird the Jewish habit of celebrating Purim each year. That theory is now untenable.

In 1890 the archaeologist Marcel Dieulafoy wrote of his discoveries at the site of the ancient Persian capital, Susa. Among other things he found prisms (dice) with the numbers 1, 2, 5 and 6 still visibly engraved on the sides. In particular, a single cube-shaped die has been found belonging to an even earlier period, dating from the time of the Assyrian King Shalmaneser III (regnum 858-824 B.C.). It bears the inscription *'puru'* (lot) on its surface, not once but twice. Known as 'the die of Iahali' (Iahali was one of Shalmaneser's officials), it was used for selecting and installing officials in Assyria. So again, those who arrogantly denounce the reliability of Scripture have been discredited no less than Haman. Esther is accurate to the smallest detail.

To this day the Jews celebrate Purim in families and in synagogues. The book of Esther is read aloud. Mordecai's name is cheered and Haman's is greeted with the stamping of feet, booing, and the grinding sound of special noisy gadgets. Private and public merriment is in order, and gifts are sent to friends and to the poor. According to some rabbis, when Messiah comes, all the other feasts of Israel will become redundant, but Purim will never cease.

Practical application

If anyone has scruples about the Christian church celebrating what is known as 'Christmas' and 'Easter', there is something to notice. God did not require Purim. It has no divine law behind it (as the feast of Passover does, for instance). But surely it is a perfectly good thing! Who would want to argue for its abandonment just because God did not command it? It is simply a yearly tradition started by godly people for godly reasons. It celebrates the mighty work of God in delivering his people from death. So it is analogous to 'Christmas' and 'Easter' in our traditions.

These are not required or commanded either. But they do not need to be. It is perfectly legitimate for Christians to gather on those traditional days (or on any other days) to declare the mighty works of God in delivering his people from death. In fact the deliverance in Christ makes the deliverance celebrated in Purim pale by comparison. It is clear to me that many Christians have an excessively restrictive view of what is historically called the Regulative Principle of Worship (RPW) as set out in chapter 21 of the *Westminster Confession of Faith*. They believe that the only things legitimate in the worship of God are those expressly commanded. So 'whatever is not commanded is forbidden'. But is that correct? If so, how can Purim stand? The initiatives of Mordecai and Esther are human not divine. There is no suggestion that Mordecai was a prophet, passing on what God first revealed to him. Additional comments on this matter are found in Appendix B.[2]

THINK ABOUT IT

We must distinguish between 'use' and 'abuse'.

Yes, there are some awful abuses and misuses of Christmas and Easter even within the visible church! But all legitimate things are misused and

WHAT THE TEXT TEACHES

abused, including food, drink, sex, preaching, prayer and praise. We do not abstain from the correct use of any good thing simply because others abuse it. Opening the doors of the church on 25 December and properly honouring God with songs of praise and the proclamation of his truth is a more practical answer to all the abuse than abstaining altogether! Think on these things.

The finishing touches

Epilogue

Undoubtedly chapter 10 (just three verses) is an epilogue written to provide a suitable end for the book. While noting that Xerxes continued his reign and continued to tax all the territories in his vast empire, we are left with the impression that it is Mordecai the Jew who is the greatest man in Persia. His role as second in charge is just like that of Joseph in Egypt 1000 years earlier: 'Mordecai the Jew was second in rank to King Xerxes, pre-eminent among the Jews, and held in high esteem by his many fellow Jews, because he worked for the good of his people and spoke up for the welfare of all the Jews' (v. 3). So who wrote this book?

Author and date?

The evidence points strongly to it being a Persian Jew, Mordecai himself being the most likely. Those who disagree usually say Mordecai would not have given himself credit at the end like that. That is satisfactorily answered by saying that Mordecai wrote the book, while a friend added the last three verses as an epilogue. The same happens today where a preface or an epilogue is added complimenting the author. Within the Bible itself there is a precedent in Deuteronomy. It was written by Moses but he did not write the epilogue (34:5-12) because it records his death and secret burial place. It was probably Joshua who added that, but it does not call into question Mosaic authorship. So the evidence suggests that Mordecai wrote the book of Esther at about 450 B.C.

Genre?

What sort of literature is it? What genre does it belong to? It is certainly historical narrative. It is narrating a story in Persia around 483 B.C. It is meant to be taken as literal historic fact. All the usual features of narrative are there: names and dates and people and places. But it is unlike any other biblical narrative. Though the author is Jewish he writes as a Persian historian or chronicler. Thus he studiously avoids advertising his religion. He avoids naming God; he makes no mention of the covenant, the law, the temple, Moses, the prophets, or the mighty acts of God. There is no mention of Israel or its sacred institutions. So Mordecai is called 'the Jew' and his people are referred to in the third person throughout (e.g. 9:15).

The writer politely avoids making explicit criticisms of King Xerxes. He lets readers draw their own opinions. He *is* openly critical of Haman and he has the support of Xerxes in this. The fact that he gives the precise names of Xerxes' counsellors (1:10,14) and the ten sons of Haman, and the exact words of the decrees posted throughout the empire, shows the author is a typical contemporary historian in Persia. Even at the end he refers the readers to other Persian sources that he is aware of: 'the book of the annals of the kings of Media and Persia' (10:2). By writing as a Persian historian the author underscores the reliability of his work. Had he openly paraded his Jewish sympathies he risked losing his credibility, especially given the main subject matter, Jewish deliverance.

Thank God for this excellent book of Esther. And thank God that Christians have even more to celebrate than Jews. Christmas and Easter celebrate more than Purim, a greater deliverance from a greater enemy by means of greater mercy. Many happy returns to you all, meaning, may every day see you joyously celebrating the victory that is everlasting in Christ.

QUESTIONS FOR DISCUSSION

1. *Why is it wise if, like the Persian Jews, we show restraint in accumulating material riches? See Proverbs 30:8-9; Matthew 19:23-24; 13:22; Luke 12:15-34; Colossians 3:5.*

2. *'Things like Christmas or eating meat are still legitimate despite having pagan-idolatrous origins.' Evaluate that in the light of 1 Corinthians 8 and Romans 14.*

3. *'Christians are always celebrating Purim.' Consider that in the light of Ephesians 1:3,7-8,18-23; Philippians 4:4; Romans 8:31-39.*

APPENDIX A

SHOULD CHRISTIANS FAST TOO?

LOOK IT UP

BIBLE READING

Esther 4:16

INTRODUCTION

It is natural for Christians to ask if we should follow Queen Esther's example when she called the Jews to fast for three days. The Lord blessed her with a good outcome. The truth is that fasting really only became common among Jews in that period of history. While fasting did occur before the exile, it was not as common as it was after the trauma of Babylon. Fasting is more frequent in the books of the exile and post-exile period. It was the fruit of discipline, the evidence of a humbled and chastened people. So naturally the question arises: 'Should we do it too?'

In the New Testament, there are instances where Christians did fast (Acts 13:3; 14:23). Jesus speaks about its misuse in his Sermon on the Mount (Matthew 6:16). Without a doubt the critical text is Matthew 9:14-15 where this very question is put to Jesus by disciples of John the Baptist: 'How is it that we and the Pharisees fast, but your disciples do not fast?' In other words, shouldn't Christians fast too? We are privileged

to have our Lord's answer. It lays down the founda-
tions for a proper understanding of fasting. It draws
the lines for the big picture, so it is imperative that we
correctly interpret his somewhat enigmatic words.

The answer

There is some value in stating the answer before setting
out the proof. Should Christians fast too? Generally,
no! Fasting in the Messianic age is not normally appropriate. It is, of course, not wrong, and not forbidden,
but it is not *normal* and not *expected*. It is much more
typical of the church in its pre-Christian form than in
its Christian form. Even in that former age, fasting was
in itself strictly neutral, non-meritorious and voluntary (except for the Day of Atonement each year).

However, therein lies the danger: since it was not
required, men began to see fasting as 'especially holy',
as a mark of religious maturity, as valuable in itself, as
exerting pressure on God, as inherently efficacious. But
Isaiah (58:5-12), Jeremiah (14:11-12) and Zechariah
(7:1-14) all spoke against those errors. So if any Christians decide to exercise their liberty to fast, it is to be a
strictly private matter between them and God, and it
should be limited. Moreover, those involved will need
to consciously guard against the inherent dangers, both
physical and spiritual. Fasting is only suitable if it helps
you to cope with life. You are not a stronger Christian
for fasting or a weaker Christian for not fasting. It may
well be the reverse. There is the answer, but now let

me show you why, by answering two further questions:

1. Why would they? (Here we consider our Lord's teaching on fasting.)
2. Why did they? (Here we consider some New Testament cases of fasting.)

Why would they?

That is exactly the answer Jesus gave when some people asked him about Christians fasting. *Why would they?* 'John's disciples came and asked him, "How is it that we and the Pharisees fast, but your disciples do not fast?" Jesus answered, "How can the guests of the bridegroom mourn while he is with them? The time will come when the bridegroom will be taken from them; then they will fast"' (Matthew 9:14-15). Notice the two parts in Jesus' answer: first, a general rule, and then an exception to the rule.

The general rule

The general rule is that Christians do not fast. Jesus says that fasting for his disciples would be completely inappropriate, just as inappropriate as refusing to celebrate with the bridegroom at his wedding. Imagine being with the bridegroom

AN EXPLANATION

on the day of his wedding, his happy day, but refusing to be happy with him. How incongruent! How out of place to be a guest at the groom's table and refuse to eat his food and drink his wine. Why would you bother accepting the invitation as his guest if you cannot enter into his joy? If you want to abstain then do not come to the banquet! In the gospel analogy, Christ is the bridegroom and Christians are his 'guests'. In fact, Christians are collectively his Bride, the Church. How can the bride sit down with her beloved and not join in the celebration? So there is the primary answer: now that Christ has come and is with us, fasting is no longer appropriate.

The exception

Jesus refers to one exception: 'The time will come when the bridegroom will be taken from them; then they will fast.' What does this mean? It is important that we get this right. When was the bridegroom taken away from his disciples? When were they right to mourn and fast? The two most plausible answers are: (1) *When he was taken away by his death,* in which case the time for fasting by Christians is long gone, lasting only three days. His resurrection ended the relevance of fasting. (2) *When he was taken away by his ascension* into heaven, in which case the time for fasting is very long, some 2000 years already, and it is still going on. Only Christ's second coming will end it. Let me show you why the first is correct and not the other.

AN EXPLANATION

First, as a matter of simple logic the second view cannot stand. It makes no sense for an exception to be far greater than the general rule itself. The time that the bridegroom had on earth with his 'guests' was only about three years. For just three years he was with them before ascending into heaven. So this 'ascension' view makes the words of Jesus mean: 'For three years the general rule is that my disciples do not fast: the only exception lasts over 2000 years when they will fast and mourn.' This reverses the whole idea of rules and exceptions. In reality, the rule would be that Christ's disciples do fast (for the whole period of church history until judgement day): the only exception is for the short time Christ was on earth with the original disciples.

To drive the point home, consider this analogy. If Christ means that fasting and mourning begins with his ascension, it is like a husband saying at his wedding: 'Today my wife and I enter into a happy covenant relationship ... she'll be in feast and celebration mode, happy and enjoying life with me. She'll certainly not be in fasting-sadness mode. The only exception will be for 99% of our married life when I'll be away. She'll be a virtual widow, though I haven't died! Then it will be appropriate for her to fast and mourn. But apart from that one 99% exception, the general expectation is that she'll be happy.' There is no logic in that.

Second, the whole drift of the New Testament sup-
ports the resurrection view. The death of Jesus came as
a dreadful calamity to the little band of men and women
who loved him. They instantly became fearful. They
went into hiding. They were in shock and mourning.
They were certainly not in 'party' mood. Just as Scripture predicted, 'Strike the shepherd and the sheep will
be scattered.' Their hopes were dashed. But the resurrection changed all that. The bridegroom was back! Not
only was he back, but over a space of forty days Jesus
filled their minds with hopes and truths that changed
them and enabled them to turn the world upside down.
He assured them that he would never be taken from
them again. He insisted he would be with them to the
very end of the age. He promised to never leave or forsake them. They would never need to fast again. They
would not need sackcloth and ashes again. He insisted
that they think of his ascension in this same way. 'It is
for your advantage that I go away. Unless I go away,
the Counsellor will not come to you; but if I go, I will
send him to you' (John 16:17).

This great day of advantage climaxed on the Day of
Pentecost. It was the advent of God. It was Christ coming
back to his church, not as he had done before in a state
of humiliation, but now in his state of exaltation. He
came to them with even greater power than his former
bodily presence, for a body can only be in one place at
one time. But through his infinite Spirit, Christ is with
his entire church in every place at every moment. It is
the age of the Spirit. And the advantage was made

immediately obvious. The gospel was proclaimed in the different languages of multitudes of eyewitnesses. One sermon was preached and 3000 people became Christians. The kingdom of Satan was being destroyed before their very eyes. Wherever believers went they spoke the gospel and turned the whole world upside down. What was the mood? It was far more like feasting than fasting: 'Every day they continued to meet together in the temple courts. They broke bread in their homes and ate together with *glad* and sincere hearts, praising God and enjoying the favour of all the people' (Acts 2:46-47).

Third, our Lord interprets his answer in John 16. This should end all disputes on the matter. Jesus has a gentle rebuke for the disciples: 'Now I am going to him who sent me, yet none of you asks me, Where are you going? Because I have said these things, you are filled with grief. But I tell you the truth: It is for your good that I am going away. Unless I go away, the Counsellor will not come to you; but if I go, I will send him to you' (vv. 5-7). So Jesus says 'grief' is the wrong attitude to have about his ascension. You should not be grieving! You should not be fasting and mourning! You should be celebrating! You should be feasting! You should be ecstatic at your blessings. Get rid of the black armbands! Sackcloth and ashes are entirely out of order now that Christ is ascended in glory. Can any words more clearly prove that these 2000 years of Christ's exaltation should have caused the church to start celebrating? How inappropriate for habitual mourning and fasting!

After describing the great work that the Holy Spirit will do for the church, Jesus returned to the matter of his ascension. "'In a little while you will see me no more, and then after a little while you will see me." Some of his disciples said to one another, "What does he mean by saying, 'In a little while you will see me no more, and then after a little while you will see me', and 'Because I am going to the Father'?" They kept asking, "What does he mean by 'a little while'? We don't understand what he is saying'" (vv. 16-18).

Now notice what happens next. 'Jesus saw that they wanted to ask him about this, so he said to them, "Are you asking one another what I meant when I said, 'In a little while you will see me no more, and then after a little while you will see me'? I tell you the truth, you will weep and mourn while the world rejoices. You will grieve, but your grief will turn to joy. A woman giving birth to a child has pain because her time has come; but when her baby is born she forgets the anguish because of her joy that a child is born into the world. So with you: Now is your time of grief, but I will see you again and you will rejoice, and no one will take away your joy'" (vv. 19-22).

Our Lord likens their present sadness to that of a woman giving birth. She does not feel like rejoicing because the anticipated blessing is not quite here. All

AN EXPLANATION

she feels is the pains leading up to it. But when the baby arrives she celebrates. She is filled with joy. So these disciples cannot bear the thought of Jesus going to heaven. They cannot bear the thought of not seeing him. 'Now is your time of grief, but I will see you again and you will rejoice, and no one will take away your joy.' *When* will this be? *When* will they see him again? *When* will they enter this state of joy and celebration? Must they wait until the second coming of Christ, his bodily return at the end of the age? Is it 2000 years and more that the sad church must cry until her joy comes? Is church history really that miserable? Not at all. The context makes it very plain that the time meant by our Lord's words 'but I will see you again and you will rejoice' is very near, just a few days away. It refers to the pouring out of the Holy Spirit after Christ ascended.

Notice how Jesus immediately defines that day in several ways. *Firstly*, he defines it in terms of their greater advantages in prayer: 'In that day you will no longer ask me anything. I tell you the truth, my Father will give you whatever you ask in my name. Until now you have not asked for anything in my name. Ask and you will receive, and your joy will be complete' (vv. 23-24). Prayer has extra dimensions through the Spirit of the risen and exalted Christ.

Secondly, he defines it in terms of the advances it will bring in the revelation of God.

'Though I have been speaking figuratively, a time is coming when I will no longer use this kind of language but will tell you plainly about my Father' (v. 25). This undoubtedly refers to the inspired writings we call the New Testament. In the New Testament Jesus continues his Messianic task as the great Prophet, revealing God the Father and his glorious will and covenant purposes. Surely no Christian would deny that revelation took giant steps forward after Christ ascended and the inspired writers composed the twenty-seven New Testament books. The New Testament 'switched on the lights for the Old Testament'. What was in the Old concealed now is in the New revealed. Shadows gave way to substance. Promise gave way to fulfilment. What was unclear on the distant horizon for Moses is now obvious on the doorstep for Christians. Even things Jesus spoke of figuratively during his earthly ministry are no longer figurative as he speaks from heaven. It is now plain, but it could only be plain when his labour was over and he entered his glory, just as any description of the mother's child could not be plain but only figurative until the labour had finished and the climax had arrived.

Thirdly, he specifically defined this day as his return to heaven: 'Father, the time has come. Glorify your Son, that your Son may glorify you ... I have brought you glory on earth by completing the work you gave me to do. And now, Father, glorify me in your presence with the glory I had with you before the world began' (17:1-5).

AN EXPLANATION

So there we have it. The only time appropriate for Christians to fast was the short time between Jesus' death and resurrection. But the resurrection of Christ and the ascension that followed have ushered in a whole new order. It is the age of the Holy Spirit, the true Vicar of Christ, the one who represents Christ in all his exalted glory and saving power. The coming of the Spirit of the risen Christ has shifted the gospel age into top gear. The sick are healed, the deaf hear, the blind see, the dead are raised to life. These are the years of Jubilee: liberty is being given to captives, debts are cancelled, lost property is restored, and rich inheritances are lavishly bestowed. The words of Isaiah have come to pass: 'There will be no more gloom for those who were in distress... The people walking in darkness have seen a great light; on those living in the land of the shadow of death a light has dawned ... they rejoice ... as people rejoice at the harvest, as men rejoice when dividing the plunder' (Isaiah 9:1-4). Fasting was typical before the light dawned but not now.

This does not mean that Christians should refuse to fast under any circumstances. But if we fast it should be driven by happier motives, conscious of the true joy of the Lord in Christ, a fast modified by a wholehearted gratitude for our most privileged position in these days of the exalted Saviour.

Why did they?

There are a few extra points to notice from other New Testament texts.

Acts 13:3; 14:23

In Acts 13 we read that the believers at Antioch fasted and prayed as they commissioned Saul and Barnabas for missionary work, and in Acts 14 the churches of Asia Minor prayed and fasted when elders were appointed. But simply quoting these texts is not conclusive. That was the age of transition between Old Testament and New Testament. There were still Apostles, it was still the age of direct revelations: 'While they were worshipping the Lord and fasting, the Holy Spirit said, "Set apart for me Barnabas and Saul for the work to which I have called them"' (13.2). They did not have the New Testament as we do. They did not know the whole counsel of God as we do. Their situation was uniquely theirs. It is dangerous to force what is simply *descriptive* in the book of Acts to make it become *prescriptive*.

Matthew 6:16-17

'When you fast, do not look sombre as the hypocrites do, for they disfigure their faces to show men they are fasting. I tell you the truth, they have received their reward in full. But when you fast, put oil on your head and wash your face, so that it will not be obvious to men that you are fasting, but only to your Father, who is unseen; and your Father, who sees what is done in secret, will reward you.' Keep in mind that Jesus is still speaking to those who were in the transition between New and Old Testament. The fact that they fasted does not imply they were obliged to fast or that Christians today should fast. *Jesus is not telling them to fast or encouraging them to do it.* He is simply saying, 'If you do fast, don't abuse it.' Don't advertise it! Don't let anyone else know about it. In other words, if we fast, it is only for our personal benefit, to help focus our minds on prayer. Jesus is echoing the words of Isaiah 58 where the fasts of Israel were denounced as useless because they were hypocritical, not accompanied by justice and righteousness. The great danger with fasting is that it inflates egos. People are inclined to think: 'He fasts regularly, what a saint.'

The other great danger with fasting is the implication that it puts pressure on God, it puts extra power into your prayers, it twists God's arm. How easy for the human mind to presume that if you pray *and* fast you have more likelihood of an answer than if you only pray. So let us be clear: fasting is not directed at God, it is directed at us. Fasting is not to influence God, but to influence us, to help us to focus more fully and devote more time in communion with God.

Conclusion

In summary, if you want to fast, do it privately. If there is a risk that you'll have to tell others about it, forget it! If you think it will make God more sympathetic to your prayers, keep eating! If it will make you feel like a more holy person, avoid it like the plague! Yes, there may be some occasions where a church might hold a day of prayer with fasting in order to focus on important issues. But let it always be understood as a totally free and voluntary thing. There should be nothing mandatory. You cannot compel people to participate. You have no right to expect church members to participate in a fast. No one should be asked, 'Why weren't you there?' We should not think less of a person who did not participate. It must never become a 'Christian Ramadan'.

Finally, it is worth noting the progress from fasting to feasting even within the book of Esther. The end result of the Jewish fast was the feast of Purim, celebrated every year after their deliverance from annihilation by Haman, 'a day of joy and feasting, a day for giving presents to each other' (9:19) because 'their sorrow was turned into joy and their mourning into a day of celebration' (9:22). So here again is the covenant pattern that Jesus declared. Fasting is appropriate for the church without her deliverance, without her bridegroom. But once the bridegroom has come and sorrow has turned to joy, the fasting gives way to feasting. This ultimate covenant pattern is foreshadowed in Esther. Feast on these things!

APPENDIX B

PERSPECTIVES ON PURIM

LOOK IT UP

BIBLE READING

What worship honours God?

INTRODUCTION

The feast of Purim, mentioned only in the book of Esther, was of human origin, not divine. Purim was not required by God. Unlike Passover, it had no divine law behind it. It was simply a yearly tradition started by God's people for a good reason: to celebrate the mighty work of God in delivering his people from death. For the 2,483 years since then it has been kept by Jews all over the world. However, it raises some questions: 'Was it a good tradition? Did it honour God? Was it acceptable to God (like the feast of Passover) even though it had no explicit warrant like Passover?' The answer is undoubtedly positive. Yes, Purim was a good thing. It honoured God. It would be an onerous task to argue for its abandonment just because God did not command it, and that it was more godly to abstain from Purim than to celebrate it.

So Purim is more than a historic fact. It is a useful index for discussing the subject of 'worship' generally and the Regulative Principle of

Worship (RPW) in particular. Purim is a good window to look at for some perspectives that apply to us today. We have already noted how Purim is analogous to 'Christmas' and 'Easter' in our traditions. These are not required or commanded either. But they do not need to be. It is perfectly legitimate for Christians to gather on those days (or on any other days) to declare the mighty works of God in delivering his people from death. In fact the deliverance in Christ makes the deliverance celebrated in Purim pale by comparison. In order to get a proper perspective, let us get to the basic principle.

What is it that lies right at the heart of this issue? What is it that regulates acceptable worship? How do we know what God accepts and what pleases him? We need to consider two things.

1. Perspectives on the question
2. Perspectives on the answer

Perspectives on the question

Private v. public worship

The New Testament distinguishes between worship 'in the church' and worship 'at home'. It distinguishes the worship of a congregation when it gathers (public worship) from the worship of individuals at other times (private worship). There are differences between the worship of God by the church body on set occasions like the Lord's Day, and the worship of God by individual members in their normal everyday living.

This distinction is particularly obvious in 1 Corinthians 11. Paul contrasts what is legitimate 'when you come together as a church' (v. 18) with what is legitimate 'at home' (v. 34). They are not the same, but the Corinthians were acting as if they were. For example, it is perfectly legitimate for prosperous Christians to eat heartily and drink the choicest foods at home. But to do it in the church, in front of poorer Christians who have little or nothing to eat, is disgraceful. The Corinthians were guilty of such behaviour when they met for a meal before the Lord's Supper. The rich ate sumptuously and the poor looked on.

Paul rebukes them: 'When you come together, it is not the Lord's Supper you eat, for as you eat, each of you goes ahead without waiting for anybody else. One remains hungry, another gets drunk. Don't you have homes to eat and drink in? Or do you despise the church of God and humiliate those who have nothing? What shall I say to you? Shall I praise you for this? Certainly not!... So then, my brothers, when you come together to eat, wait for each other. If anyone is hungry, he should eat at home, so that when you meet together it may not result in judgement'

AN EXPLANATION

(vv. 20-22,33-34). Clearly, different considerations regulate each sort of worship. What is valid worship of God at home may be invalid in the church and vice versa. Keep this perspective in mind.

What regulates private worship?

Regarding worship in the broader sense (all of life), it is clear that what regulates it is the whole revealed will of God (Scripture). The Bible is the supreme standard for all of faith and life, and nothing is to be done which is inconsistent with the Bible. The Bible is a clear and sufficient guide to regulate the behaviour of any person and to 'equip him for *every* good work' (2 Timothy 3:17). So the Pauline injunction sums it up: 'whatever you do [in every aspect of life] work at it with all your heart, as working for the Lord' (Colossians 3:23,17). In other words, we do not need a specific command to authorize how we worship in our everyday lives. Is there anything inherently unbiblical about such activities as using a computer, swimming in the surf, climbing a mountain, digging for gold, writing a book, dancing, rehearsing a drama or playing golf? No! Are they within the boundaries set by Scripture? Of course! So they are allowable things, and if done with a right attitude they are pleasing to God. This is not really a point of debate within orthodox Christianity, but as to the regulation of worship 'in the church', that is a different matter, to which we now turn.

AN EXPLANATION

What regulates public worship?

Churches worldwide have answered that in the *Westminster Confession of Faith*:

> The acceptable way of worshipping the true God is instituted by Himself, and so limited by His own revealed will that He may not be worshipped according to the imaginations and devices of men, or the suggestions of Satan, under any visible representation, or any other way not prescribed in the Holy Scripture (WCF 21).

This is what we call 'The Regulative Principle'. It is difficult to see how any sincere Christian can disagree with this, especially Protestants. This was at the very heart of the Protestant Reformation in the sixteenth century. However, a problem *does* arise when we come to the precise application of that principle. What exactly is 'instituted' and 'prescribed' by God? What exactly does his revealed will 'limit' us to? Within the family of Protestant Reformed churches, two different approaches exist, which, for the sake of discussion, can be called *The Commandment View*, and *The Consistency View*. They differ as follows:

1. *The Commandment View* believes that you must have a commandment for anything and

everything that you do when the church assembles to worship God. Whatever is commanded is obligatory. Failure to obey it is sin. But, if a given act is not explicitly commanded, it is forbidden. No matter how beneficial that activity may be, or how reasonable it might be on all other grounds, if it lacks commandment it lacks permission. The voice of silence is the voice of prohibition. The words 'instituted ... limited ... prescribed' are taken in the same sense, namely, *instituted* by way of commandment, *limited* to what is commanded, *prescribed* by way of commandment.

There is much that is compelling and attractive about this view. It certainly makes it easy to sort out if we should or should not do a certain thing in the worship of the church. All you have to do is find out if it is commanded or not. If it is, you not only *may* do it, but you *must* do it. Otherwise you must *not* do it. It is a very safe policy in that it certainly prevents innovations creeping into Christian worship. However, is that really the right way to understand the *Westminster Confession*? Or, more to the point, is that what Scripture teaches? No, there is a second view that is more commendable to the vast majority of Reformed churches.

2. *The Consistency View* believes that each aspect of 'public worship' must be consistent with the whole of Scripture, and must take notice of the radical differences between Old and New Testament worship. The problem with the 'commandment' view is that it fails to allow for the symbolic and temporary nature of pre-Christian worship. We must remember that when the

AN EXPLANATION

Old Testament church (Israel) assembled, it was not simply 'worship' as we know it. It was nothing less than a dramatic role-play of the gospel. The gospel was acted out in the ceremonial drama, the shadowy symbols of Christ. There was bloodshed, there were scapegoats, there were altars, and there were innocent victims slain. There were the priests, rituals, temples and atonements. The details of Old Testament worship were minute and numerous, right down to the size and shape of the meeting place (tabernacle) and the sorts of timbers and fabrics to be used. The punishment for disregarding these things was harsh because the whole liturgy was typical of Christ and his work (worship). Therefore everything had to be regulated by divine command. To stop short of what God commanded or to add one little extra was not merely changing 'worship', it was far more serious. It would be changing what those ceremonies pointed to, namely, changing the *gospel*! It would be man tampering with the perfect work of Christ in its Old Testament preview. (Those living at the time did not understand this, of course.)

The 'commandment view' of worship was true for the church *prior* to the coming of Christ. But that is not the case now. The symbols and shadows are all fulfilled in Christ. This is what the letter to the Hebrews is all about. There is a radical discontinuity. The worship of the assembled church is no longer a dramatic role-play of the gospel where every detail counts and where there are no liberties or 'things indifferent'. Our worship is not a ceremonial prefiguring of the Messiah. Our worship glories in the finished details, the fulfilment of perfect, pure, 'down to the smallest detail' worship in Christ. Christ is the only pure worshipper. Christ offered both perfect 'whole of life worship' and perfect 'ceremonial-priestly-atoning worship'.

The altar has gone: it was the cross! The priests and sacrifices have gone in Christ! Sins have been remitted once for all because the precious blood of the Lamb of God has been accepted in the heavens, the real 'Holy of Holies' made without human hands! We enjoy the liberty of the church that has come of age, having collected its inheritance in the Father's will. We are no longer bound and regulated by the strictures of a child (study carefully Galatians 3:17 - 4:31). We must, as a mature adult, make decisions that will please God in the light of all that we know of him, not ignoring the progress of redemption. We are not locked into the same strictures as the Jews of that era. That is the point Paul labours. Those are the perspectives on the question.

Perspectives on the answer

Consider Corinth

The best perspective is gained from 1 Corinthians 14. There Paul is regulating the things done 'in the church'

AN EXPLANATION

at Corinth. How did he do that? What regulating principle did he use? It certainly needed regulating because there was great disorder and it certainly bore little resemblance to the Old Testament worship. For example, there was *glossalalia* (tongue speaking). How did Paul regulate that? (It is not my purpose now to prove these tongues no longer apply today, that's another issue.) Which view of 'The Regulative Principle' does Paul use in Corinth? Did he take the strict Old Testament view? Does Paul simply ask them: 'Where is the commandment in Scripture to speak in tongues? Where has God sanctioned these tongues?'

If Paul had used that approach, there would have been no speaking in tongues, for the simple reason that *nowhere* in the whole Bible does God *command* tongue-speaking (otherwise, every church must have a 'tongues' segment in its programme or be guilty of disobedience). By that strict view 'tongues' would be forbidden! But Paul actually says, 'Do not forbid speaking in tongues' (v. 39). So a very big change has taken place. Something that has not been commanded anywhere in Scripture is now allowed in the church! In fact, the only thing forbidden is the forbidding of what was never commanded. And even before Paul gave them this sanction they were still not sinning in the act of tongue-speaking. So, clearly, the second view of 'The

Regulative Principle' is correct. All that we do in the
assemblies of the church must be consistent with Scripture as an entirety. Notice that there are five main
aspects to this New Testament Regulative Principle. For
any activity to be allowed 'in the church':

a. it must be edifying (v. 26 and stated repeatedly)
b. it must be temperate and not overdone (v. 27)
c. it must be orderly and decorous (vv. 29-33)
d. it must not violate male headship and oversight
   (v. 34)
e. it must be consistent with apostolic writings
   (vv. 37-38)

So the RPW cannot be reduced down to just one
single issue: Is it commanded? Rather it embraces several issues: Is it edifying? Is it temperate? Is it orderly?
Is it according to God-given rules of headship? Is it
apostolic? So we believe that the Bible authorizes the
following activities in the worship of the assembled
church (grouped in three categories for convenience):

1. Prayer, reading and preaching of the Bible, singing
praise to God, baptism and Lord's Supper (the *Westminster Confession* calls these 'all parts of the ordinary
religious worship of God').

2. On special occasions, taking solemn oaths and vows
(inducting and ordaining elders, commissioning
missionaries), fasting and thanksgiving.

3. Such other things as meet all the regulating principles in the New Testament, especially the requirements in 1 Corinthians 14 and Colossians 2:16-23.

Above all, we believe that the faithful preaching of God's Word is the central activity in congregational worship, and all the other activities must be seen in that light. The preached word must never be diminished, upstaged, mitigated, or in any way forced to make way for other things (no matter how good they may be).

Where does this leave us?

It means that the elders will have to consider any given activity on its merits before it is permitted in the worship of the church. There is no 'list' in Scripture setting out what is allowed and what is not. It is neither a simple matter of forbidding whatever is not commanded, nor of concluding that 'anything goes' or that anything which can be shown to have pleased God in the past is allowed. These are extreme views that do not harmonize with the 'big picture' painted in Scripture. Each case calls for a wise and carefully reasoned application of the principles defended above. Should we allow drama, or solo renditions of songs, or news and notices, or puppets, or pageants, or missionary deputations, or slides and videos and films? What about children's messages, and memorizing Bible verses? The list is large.

It all depends on satisfying the principles in 1 Corinthians 14. So, does it edify? That is a very different question to 'Do you enjoy it, does it move you emotionally?', or even 'Can you interpret a message out of it?' Edification in the New Testament sense means almost the same as the *Westminster Confession of Faith* means by 'with understanding'. Does it instruct the rational faculty of man? Is it building up the mind to maturity in Christ? Does it convey plain, coherent, logical thoughts to help us think God's thoughts after him?

Paul uses a very simple rule of thumb in these matters. Suppose a complete stranger comes into the church and witnesses your preaching or praying, for example. And suppose he is an unbeliever with no understanding about Christ and gospel. Would he be edified? Would he 'be convicted by all and called to account as the secrets of his heart are revealed'? Would he 'fall on his face and worship God, declaring that God is certainly among you'? Or would he be so unsure of exactly what the point is that he concludes: 'You are mad'? That is the test (1 Corinthians 14:23-26). Paul is not necessarily opposed to tongues or certain other things, but he will never use tongues in the church (and he was more gifted than all of them in that, too) when a few plain edifying words will do better (vv. 18-19). Therefore, by applying this same rule, we understand that he would not sanction anything in the church to 'teach' some

AN EXPLANATION

gospel truth when plain words will do the job much more effectively.

Finally, the opinions of the elders might differ from the opinions of some members in the church. That will always happen on some issues. The point is that law and order must prevail and it is not the members of the church who are charged by God to attend to it: it is the elders. We must always respect and defend the rights of each person to have liberty of conscience (*Westminster Confession of Faith*, ch. 20). And they must always defer to the lawful oversight of the eldership. Our conclusions may differ from other denominations or even other congregations in the same church. But we can do that without condemning them as heretical or liberal! We should defend our views firmly with biblical logic, without thinking that those who differ in conscience are inferior. What is truly alarming and reprehensible is when churches or individuals dismiss the biblical principles about worship, and refuse to invest the careful scholarship and agony of thought needed before arriving at conclusions. It hardly needs proving that pragmatic and slipshod decision-making is widespread in modern Christendom.

THE GUIDE

NOTES

NOTES

Chapter 1

1. Persia became Iran in 1935. The remains of the ancient capital Susa (Shushan) are still identifiable today, in the form of a mound of ruins 200 miles north of the Persian Gulf. The location, identified by scholars in 1852, has been excavated twice: in 1884-86, and in 1946-51.

The 70-year exile of the Jews in Babylon ended when the Medo-Persian Empire displaced Babylon. In 539 B.C. Cyrus the Mede decreed that the Jews were free to return to Palestine. The setting of the book of Esther is some 50-60 years later. The king is Ahasuerus (Xerxes I, 486-465 B.C.), the son and successor of King Darius I. Haggai had rebuilt the temple in Jerusalem at the beginning of Darius' reign, completing it in 516 B.C. Confirmation of the historical information is remarkably good because the Greek historian Herodotus wrote in this very period of Esther.

The LXX gives the king's name as *Artaxerxes* throughout, which might imply Artaxerxes II (404-359 B.C). However the facts are clarified by recent diggings at the ruins of Persepolis, which have identified this king in three different languages.

In Greek he is *Xerxes*, in Persian he is Darius's son *Khshayarsha*, and in Babylonian he is *Adhashwerosh*, which is nearly identical to his Hebrew name Ahasuerus אֲחַשְׁוֵרוֹשׁ.

His son was King Artaxerxes whom Nehemiah served as his cup-bearer some forty years later. Persian kings rotated their residential palaces between Susa, Persepolis, Ecbatana and Babylon.

Susan was only used in winter because of its extreme heat otherwise.

Chapter 2
1. That is the thesis of a recent book *The Surrendered Wife* by American Laura Doyle, published in Australia in June 2001 by Simon & Schuster. It represents an excessive response to radical feminism.

Chapter 3
1. Assassination of kings was common in the ancient Near East. One Israelite king after another suffered it (Nadab, 1 Kings 15:27; Elah, 16:9-10; Joram, 2 Kings 9:14-24; Zechariah and Pekahiah, 15:10,25; Amon, 21:23). It happened to the king of Damascus (2 Kings 8:15), Assyria (2 Kings 19:37) and eventually to Xerxes himself in a similar plot fourteen years later.

Chapter 4
1. See for instance Joyce Baldwin in *Esther* (Tyndale Commentary, IVP 1984, pp.72,73,76).
2. Sir Arthur Sullivan, 1871. No. 678, *Trinity Hymnal*, hymnbook of the Orthodox Presbyterian Church of America.

Chapter 5
1. No. 408, *Rejoice*, hymnbook of the Presbyterian Church of Australia.
2. No. 474, *Rejoice*. Based on the earlier hymn of William Pioroon Morrill (1807-1954), as found in the Church of Scotland's *Revised Christian Hymnal*.

Chapter 8
1. It is not my task here to develop the issue of legitimate self-defence. Related issues like gun laws need to be biblically assessed. Christians should not let humanists

and politicians do our thinking for us. Once the right for self-defence is granted, the issue of weapons becomes vital. Is there any point in allowing self-defence for unarmed citizens? What protection do bare hands afford against gun-toting criminals? The issue cannot be avoided by saying, 'I just trust in God to protect me. He has promised to be my shield, my fortress, my hiding place, my high tower.' Esther and the Jews did not resort to such pietistic escapism, denying human responsibility.

Chapter 9

1. Bruce W. Jones, 'Two Misconceptions about the Book of Esther', *Catholic Bible Quarterly* 39, 1977, p. 180.

Chapter 10

1. Reckoning from 483 B.C. to A.D. 2001.
2. Some may consider that Christmas and Easter, being of pagan origin, are not really analogous with Purim which has a godly origin in the OT church. Even so, other considerations must be kept in mind. Many things which are part and parcel of our daily Christian lives have a pagan origin. Even the days of the week are named after pagan idols. If we try to remove all pagan historical elements from day-to-day life we'll have to leave the planet! It is impossible! No one can turn back the clock. And it is not just on 25 December when pagans worship idols and act in ignorance. They do it every day of the year. That is no argument against Christians honouring the true God on any day. We are in real trouble if we are only prepared to preach the gospel in those days and seasons left moderately unpaganized by Satan and his hordes.

A wide range of excellent books on spiritual subjects is available from Evangelical Press. Please write to us for your free catalogue or contact us by e-mail.

Evangelical Press
Faverdale North Industrial Estate, Darlington, DL3 0PH, England

Evangelical Press USA
P. O. Box 84, Auburn, MA 01501, USA

e-mail: sales@evangelicalpress.org

web: www.evangelicalpress.org